A Room
Without Roaches
Please

DR. JOANN HOWELLS

authorHOUSE®

AuthorHouse™
1663 Liberty Drive
Bloomington, IN 47403
www.authorhouse.com
Phone: 1-800-839-8640

Published by AuthorHouse   05/08/2012

ISBN: 978-1-4670-7109-3 (sc)
ISBN: 978-1-4670-7108-6 (e)

Library of Congress Control Number: 2011962957

ACKNOWLEDGEMENT

This book was a dream of mine to be published one day. A dream has become a reality through a special Angel that has been put into my life.

Thru Kathy Doneghey's kindness and many, many hours dedicated to aiding me in completing this manuscript. It is now going to publication!

Kathy, it is indeed, an Angel, always willing to step in, not only making my dream possible but others dreams possible with her unselfishness and giving heart. I remind Kathy that she truly is a gift to me!

Thank you my Angel,
JoAnn

FOREWORD

This book is dedicated to the many clients I have seen in private practice, psychiatric hospitals, street ministry and the Supreme Court in Brooklyn.

I have entitled it "A Room Without Roaches, Please", to address many clients who have suffered physical, emotional and financial abuse as a direct or indirect result of their low self-esteem.

People should not let others bring poison into their lives or homes, via phone or internet.

I consider my clients "Broken Sparrows" who have suffered at the hand of poisonous playmates and vicious perpetrators, some among the clergy, as indicated in my chapter on priest abuse.

If one person is helped by reading this book, my mission on earth is complete.

THE FUNERAL

A hush fell over the flower-scented room as people filed silently up to the casket. There lay all my broken dreams and unfulfilled desires. He was so still and I noticed the undertaker had not done a good job on his make-up. Another woman staggered up to the casket, sobbing hysterically. Next in line were his four children. All I could do was sit there in frozen anger and sorrow. The thief, alcohol, had stolen my husband from me. Alcohol had ravished and raped my home, depriving my children of their father.

The sobbing woman he lived with was just another testimony of the broken promises of his life and the lives he had ruined. Two more children calling him "Daddy" added to the mourning scene. Now the secret was out in the open. Neither family was aware of the other. Enter his sisters, Bea and Edith, whom he had cast aside as well for thirty-five years. They too cried for the brother they never had.

His barroom friends came and said inane things like, "It's a nice funeral . . . he looks good." I tried to ponder how you look good "dead". People mean well, but they say empty words. I was sure this nightmare of a funeral would never end.

Walking slowly up to the casket, I saw another woman approaching me. She was the woman he had lived with for many years. She wanted to talk to me and tell me that they were watching television and eating when he was seized with chest pains. They were both drunk and by the time the ambulance arrived and got him to the hospital, he was brain dead. Death had cast its shadow and their good times were over. The hospital had him hooked up with life supports and kept trying to resuscitate him at my children's request. My children were holding hands at this bedside, praying for him. Maria, my oldest son Ricky's

1

wife, and her sister came to pay their respects to him. They both needed closure because he had raped both of them at an earlier time when tbaby-sitting for his girl friends. All I saw as I gazed around that sterile hospital room were broken little sparrows, wounded children and grandchildren who were praying for a man who had discarded them thirty-five years ago.

I was employed in the court system at this time, not far from the hospital. My boss was a wonderful, understanding man who gave me extended lunch hours to visit my dying husband. He just wouldn't die until my last son, Robert, and his wife arrived from North Carolina. We were all subjected to watch him, hooked up to machines, not able to talk or to recognize any of us. Daily visits to this scene were wearing us down. He had not been home or given support for thirty-five years. I was left with four children to starve with no compassion from him for us. My dream home had become a boarding house. Renting rooms was the only way I could survive and keep my family from becoming homeless. My coworkers advised me not to visit him.

My job in the court system was working with "high-risk" felons on an alternate sentencing program. I had to make house calls in the most dangerous areas in Brooklyn to the client's families, write pre-sentencing reports for the judge, testify at their trials, and attempt to modify their behaviors. My husband was dying only ten minutes away from my job. The job was my salvation because it took me out of myself and my own troubles. It allowed to help other people in worse situations than mine, such as facing jail time for crimes. Each time I visited my husband, the doctor would approach me to take him off the life supports. One night, I asked a visiting priest to give him the Last Rites of the Catholic Church. However, I could not bring myself to take him off the life supports until I had consulted with my children.

At last, I believe God saw that we had enough suffering. I left the hospital to consult with my children and when I got home, my daughter called and said he had died. God had made that decision for me. My husband had made a lot of money in the shipping industry, but he spent it on women and alcohol. Now, at the end of his life, neither he, nor his girlfriend had any money to bury him. In my other life as a waitress, I worked long hours to support four children and grandchildren. I found an old insurance policy that I had paid until I could no longer pay it. There was some money left in this policy totaling four thousand dollars. I was in school at the time and did not want to part with this new found money for his funeral.

I had joined a prayer group, which was formed in the court system, and we met once a week. We also went to Grand Central Station to help the homeless. My co-workers told me to keep the money and let him go to Potter's Field. However, I did not want my children to suffer. I held the check in my hand and went to my prayer group. They would not advise me, but told me to put the check on the table. They laid hands on it and prayed. I knew then that I would give the check to his sister to pay for his funeral.

Final arrangements were made. His sister, Bea, and my husband's girlfriend had a tug of war over where the wake was to be held. Brooklyn was where his drinking friends were. Huntington was close to his sister's home. Huntington won! My son Ricky paid $160 for a funeral Mass. The priest gave my name as the deceased. My daughter screamed, "It's not my mother who is dead, it's my father!" She was "dead" wrong. I died the day I married him. On that fateful day, at my mother's insistence on a Catholic marriage, the young girl I used to be had ceased to exist.

MOTHER AND DAD

Taking a walk back in time, I saw a little girl sleeping on a loveseat. There wasn't a bed for her to sleep in. Mother and Dad had the bedroom. Early in the game of life, I had the impression that I didn't count. You can speck about low self-esteem, but I carried and image of "no self-esteem". Mother and Dad came from Ireland to this so-called "Land of Opportunity". They arrived at Ellis Island, only to find out that the streets were not paved in gold. The stock market had crashed and the streets were lined with bodies. Mother had been a baby-trained nurse, and Dad had sung in the Metropolitan Opera House. Those days were over, as survival was the theme in the Depression years.

They moved to Dean Street, Brooklyn, where my sister, Maryellen was born. Dad had to take a job as a waiter to support his family. As he leaned over each table, waiting on stockbrokers, no one saw the song in his heart. The family moved to Sunnyside, Long Island. I believe Mother wanted to be near her brother, Harry. I was born there, at home. Later on in years, I was told what a horrible birth it was. Daddy passed out as I entered this world. My father was a heart broken, depressed man. He was so tuned into my mother's alcoholism that he had no time for my sister and me in his life. I was told how much suffering I caused my mother when she gave birth to me. At my birth, Daddy was no help. I think, in some ways, this explains his indifference to me. Later on, after my marriage at 16, I learned I was married to my "father". My spouse, Dick, never said, "I love you". Neither did my father.

I lived a lonely, isolated life as a child. There was no one to talk to. My sister was 18 years older than I was, so we were never close. As my mother was usually drunk, I tried to find a mother substitute in my older, mentally ill sister. Life was a living nightmare. I have early childhood memories of my sister jumping out of closets calling herself "Gladys". Looking back, I can see her Schizophrenia, which was diagnosed at a later date. She delighted in my screaming and crying with fear. Then she would become my "nice" sister, Maryellen. "Muriel" was another personality that emerged during these tortuous sessions. I used to beg my mother not to leave me alone with her. One day when Mother and Dad went to a mass to attend my grandfather's wake, I was left alone with my sick sister and her multiple personalities. The whole time my parents were gone, I lived in mortal fear. There was no one to turn to for help. When Mother and Dad came home they never mentioned my grandfather or how he died. Family secrets!

My Dad had cashed his dreams of being a singer to wait on tables in a Wall Street restaurant. No one saw the song in his heart. Mother always belittled my father because he was a waiter. She used to make him wear a suit and pack his tuxedo in a bag so the neighbors did not see what he did for a living. I always felt that I was a burden and it was my fault that my mother drank and my parents argued. A sense of powerlessness and futility were heavy burdens for a young child to carry. I never felt wanted and since there was 18 years difference between my sister and me, I am sure my parents were not waiting expectantly for another child.

I was a sickly child and doctors were to discover later as I was growing up that I only had one kidney. A doctor said that it was possible I was once of a pair of twins, and that the other twin had aborted. One lived and one died. Did I live or did I die? Growing up in this crazy, dysfunctional atmosphere of poverty and alcoholism did not contribute to make me a healthy child. I was a very isolated, lonely child, and I did not make friends very easily. I did have one friend, Sammy. He was a turtle, and my little pet. I trained him to eat out of my hand. One day I went to say hello to him and he was dead. I cried my eyes out, but no one heard me.

PRE-SCHOOL YEARS

My pre-school years were spent in isolation. At this point in my life, I would wake up screaming with nightmares. Since I would dream I was losing my soul, my mother who said the rosary in between her drinking bouts, was frightened into sobriety. She would then take me into her bed and I thought this was a great privilege, since I slept on that small loveseat in the living room. If I closed my eyes as I write this, I can see her bedroom—a small dark room with a statue of the Sacred Heart over the twin beds. I adored my mother and spent most of my life trying to make her life better. I used to follow her wherever she went. One of our "tribal rituals" was weekly confession and Sunday mass. Mother would come out of the confessional and say that the priest said she had no sins. This confused me because she drank every day. On our daily walks to the liquor store, my mother would stop and talk to neighbors. I used to pull at her hand, because in these sober moments I did not want to share her with anyone. The sober moments were too rare and precious to me. The man in the liquor store knew that my mother wanted "Shenley's", and this recognition was a source of delight for my mother. My poor, sick mother felt honored when he said, "Mrs. Gallagher, here is a calendar for you". On our way home from the liquor store I would hold her hands tightly, because I knew I would soon lose her to the "coma" which followed her consumption of the alcohol.

Another tribal ritual, when the Shenley's was gone, was my mother's bath. After her bath, I was told to use the bath water. I was never sure why, because we did not have to pay for the water or the heat. My sister would freak out at this "ritual" but I made jokes about it saying it was the water of "Lourdes" containing a miracle cure. But I never really

6

talked about this to anyone; it was a source of shame to me. Since my mother could do no harm, I followed her orders.

We had another ritual after the bath. I was given an enema to "clean me out". Hence, the title, "A Room without Roaches, Please". I always felt dirty.

Daddy would come home late at night and wake me up to tell me his life story. He had some bad breaks in life, but at 2:00am in the morning, I didn't care too much. Since I did not have my own room, there was no escaping his waking me to tell me about his life. He was a heart-broken, depressed man, who had traded in his dreams to live a sad life with an alcoholic wife. Later on in life I learned Daddy was using me as his therapist. He could not face the fact that my mother was an alcoholic because he was one too.

He used to cry and ask me what he should do about Mama's drinking. I told him that I heard a program on the radio that said people with problems could be helped by joining an organization called Alcoholics Anonymous. When he told my mother what I had said, there was "hell to be paid". Mama was very angry with me. It seemed as though they both turned against me.

My mother was drunk every night, and I used to have terrible nightmares. She had a friend, Peggy Kite, who would visit her. Peggy was also an alcoholic, and drank with my mother our small kitchen. When my mother passed out, Peggy went home. When Mama woke up, she would take me with her into her bed. The smell of stale alcohol would make me sick. Sometimes, my mother would wake up and spit in my face. Is it any wonder I had no self-esteem? My inheritance was a pain-filled life.

One day, when Peggy came to visit, she brought her son, Tommy and asked Mama to baby-sit for her. Poor little Tommy did not know what he was in for. Mama put out all the lights and passed out. Tommy was left on his own for dinner. I was too afraid to do anything to help him, since Mama held me in a death grip on the couch. Peggy never left her son in Mama's care again.

SCHOOL DAYS

At about 6 years of age, my mother took me to #125 Public School to register me for Kindergarten. My first day at school was a dark, dreary day. The school was like a prison. I was imprisoned by my loneliness and fears. I felt abandoned by Mama. Drunk or sober, I really loved my little, Irish mother. The principal had Mama take me out of the class and the school. They did not know what to do with such a sickly child.

Mama took me to St. Theresa's School, and I was admitted to first grade. A little nun, Sister Miriam Edward taught this class. There was an aura about her that spoke of her holiness. I did very well in my grade because I loved this nun. I studied very hard and received high grades. There were no toys or books in my home. Money was spent on alcohol. I remember a neighbor gave me a Princess Elizabeth doll as a gift. Mama told me that they just gave me the doll in appreciation for how good she was to their mother. I was not allowed to play with the doll, only to look at it. Then the doll was put back in the box. However, on another occasion, I was given a doll and a doll carriage from some relatives. I loved to play "house" with the doll and pretend I was the mother.

My sister was somewhere in the picture during this time, but I don't know where she slept. I only remember she was very ashamed of my mother and father. When her boyfriend came to pick her up, Daddy's long johns were hanging on our clothesline in the kitchen, my mother was usually drunk and my father was not home. My poor, sick sister used to buy the New York Times to try to convince her boyfriend that the family read the paper. She always tried to create an illusionary world. Eventually, as you will see later in the story, she retreated into this illusionary world of hers.

School days, school days! They were happy days because I was away from the horror scene at home. We began our day at St. Theresa's by lining up in the schoolyard, and then class-by-class attended daily mass. I could not wait to receive Jesus in the Holy Communion. I was a very religious child. I aspired to be a nun when I grew up. Catholic school had it's many advantages, and also disappointments. The nuns told us stories about the saints. My favorite story was about Father Damien who went to the island of Molokai, to work with the lepers. In those days, I had a missionary spirit, and I wanted to work with lepers too.

The nuns encouraged us to make Easter and Christmas cards with our Spiritual Bouquets, which consist of praying Hail Mary's and out Father's as well as Act of Charity for our family. My Easter cards were full of prayers and Acts of Charity toward my neighbors also. I was a very quiet child and I studied very hard. My days were spent in constant worry about what I would find when I got home. Mama used to walk me to school, and come back at lunchtime to take me out for lunch. We wore a school uniform with a white collar and cuffs/ Mama used to change my cuffs at lunchtime. She meant well, but the alcohol always defeated her. On one of her trips to school, a car hit her. My teacher, Sister Maria Beatrice told me, but she said Mama was not hurt. We never spoke about that—another family secret.

MY FIRST COMMUNION

The time had come for me to receive Jesus, whom I longed for. We made our First Confession at 7 years old. I confessed all my thoughts and deeds. I was very hard on myself, never sparing myself or making any excuses for my behavior. I really had no sins at all. However, we were taught that "everything" was a sin. Venial sins were a less offense, but a mortal sin was a sentence to Hell.

Father McCloud was my favorite confessor. He also gave me my First Communion. In those youthful days, nuns and priests could do no wrong. Mother and I went to Confession weekly. I was a scrupulous penitent. Mother would come out of the confessional and say that Father McCloud said she had no sins. This was confusing to me since she was always drunk. My poor, deluded mother knew nothing about alcoholism, and neither did I. She was a very lonely person who tried to fill a hole in her soul with alcohol. My father was a silent martyr who was never at home. He too had the "Irish Virus".

My First Communion was a happy day for me, despite the fact that my white dress was a hand-me-down from my cousin, Marie. The image of myself as "a little girl in the white Communion dress" was to follow me all my life. Someone took a picture of me and when that picture would turn up, it reminded me of whom I used to be. I refer to it as my "other life". My school days after my First Communion were spent studying very hard. I was always on the Honor Roll. However, my mathematics was not so good. So Mama suggested that her brother, Uncle Harry, help me. He would come to our house, which was 4 blocks from his. My math improved and so did my Uncle's lust for me.

I was a silent, withdrawn child. However, I did go to daily Mass and Communion. I went to Confession for Father McCloud. I was so strict with myself, that if I forgot one so-called sin after he gave me absolution, I would get back in the long lines, and wait to confess this sin. How you can commit sins at age 7 still amazes me! Since my home life was a living nightmare, I went to the rectory to see Father McCloud, whom I had complete trust in. I told him about my mother's alcoholism and how she would spit in my face. I only told him because I wanted to help my father, you see, I had no self-esteem. Father McCloud called a meeting with my father and mother. I was not involved in the conversation.

After my mother and father took me home, I was told that I was a traitor, and dme my family. My father said I had bit the hand that fed me. This was another contradiction to me since my father was also telling me his problems with my mother. I only tried to help, but was to pay a higher price of misery no, as life at home became hell-on-earth. My nights were spent in a fitful sleep on a loveseat too small to accommodate me, as I was getting taller. My days in school were a welcome release and a good escape. I was very obedient and an honor student, with high academics in grammar school despite condition at my home.

The neighborhood I lived in was a dark, dreary prison-like environment owned by Metropolitan Life Insurance Company. There was a large courtyard connecting the buildings. We would play in the courtyard, and like me, most of my playmates were in the low-income bracket. I was a lonely, isolated child and did not mix well. The other kids made fun of my mother. She had dyed her hair red, and they said if it rained, her hair would fade. I was very ashamed of my mother and father. My father was a silent, withdrawn man, who was never home.

My playmates and I used to ring bells and run and hide. Once, we rang a lady's bell so much, that when her husband came home, she refused to let him in.

CONFIRMATION

Another tribal ritual we observed was confirmation. I received confirmation in my cousin's hand me down dress. At this sacrament, the Bishop smacked our face to signify that we would die for our faith. At this time I was having terrible nightmares. I would wake up screaming thinking that I lost my soul. One of my worst fears was that my Mama would die. When she was drunk, she went into a coma like status and I was fearful and lost in my loneliness. I did not deal with these fears but I went to Mass and Communion. I believed that this was the answer to all my problems.

My parents and my relatives referred to me as a silent scared child. They used to say, "She's afraid of her own shadow." I never spoke or played with anyone. Those secrets that we keep are shame based. The lonely lost child wandering the earth was always wanting to make things better. I not only had low self-esteem, I had no self-esteem. Thus the title "A Room Without Roaches, Please".

I was getting taller now and sleeping on a small, love seat in the living room. It was very uncomfortable. Mother and Daddy slept in the bedroom. When Daddy came home at night he liked to drink beer and wake me up to tell me about his terrible life with an overly strict father. He left his home in Massachusetts and found himself on the Bowery in New York sleeping in a 25 cent-a-night room. I can only assume that he felt my life was luxurious compared to his. After listening to his confessions, I had to get up early for school. I was happy that Daddy spoke to me despite these sad tales. The next day, I went to school very tired. The Dominican nuns who taught us were so removed from reality that you didn't dare tell them about your life. My school days in St. Theresa's were fear filled. I lived in daily fear of what I would find when I came home from school. One day I came home early and found my Mama passed out on the love seat. I got hysterical and put a mirror to her mouth to see if she was dead. Relieved she was only drunk and in a stupor, I buried the pain and felt it was my fault. I never mentioned this incident and hoped I was having a bad dream. Later, Mama was really scared and she went to the store and bought me a comic book. This was a rarity since we did not even have newspapers or books.

Daddy came home from work and found Mama drunk again, blamed me. I failed in my task to stop my Mama's drunkenness. I accepted this blame and shame, and carried guilt most of my life. I tried to find her alcohol, but she was very skilled at hiding it.

My nightmares continued and one night I work up screaming and I couldn't breathe. Mama said there was a gas leak from an old refrigerator. In my dreamy, semi-conscious state, I saw an old man in a black suit. He was coming to take my soul to Hell. I was already there in my home. Mother woke me up but I felt like my lungs were full of gas. The next day, I went to school and made believe everything was fine. I had to borrow a red skirt to go to school. My uniform smelled of gas. That day my red skirt was filled with blood. Sister Helen Theresa sent me to the bathroom with a schoolmate, Jean Courtney, to clean me up. I was sent home. I did not know what was happening to me and the nun was silent. When I got home, my sister explained to me that now I was a woman. I still was not sure what she was talking about. I was only thankful that I didn't bleed to death.

Things were getting worse at home. I used to clean up Mama's messes, so Daddy wouldn't know what happened. I was old when I was young. My mother's favorite name for me was Slow Motion, and another Irish put down was Amathon, which means stupid. My role as a child was confused because I became my mother's mother. Daddy came home from working as a waiter, to blame me for not taking care of my mother. I believe he was bitter about his life and felt burdened with the cross he was carrying.

Mama was losing control of her kidneys now, since her disease was progressing. I know now, having more knowledge about alcoholics, that my mother was in blackouts. My poor lonely Mama used to like to visit my Aunt Vera who lived in Brooklyn. Aunt Vera was a lively, vivacious woman who had married three times. Her first husband was my mother's stepbrother, Joe, and he was the love of her life. She married at a very young age and gave birth to Delores, who was born mildly retarded. Uncle Joe died very suddenly and this left Aunt Vera with no money and a child to raise.

Aunt Vera got a job as a ticket taker in the subways and one night she was raped and robbed on her way home from work. At this time she met a man whom we called Uncle Jack and he fell madly in love with her and married her. Uncle Jack was a really charming, loving man. He made great fuss over me and gave me the love I never got at home. He and Aunt Vera were proud of me and took me to the local bars to show me off. He wanted to but Aunt Vera the world, but unfortunately, he drank a bit too much and fell into heavy debt. He forged some checks and the law caught up with him. He wrote Aunt Vera a letter telling her he was sorry and jumped to his death from the Saint George Hotel in Brooklyn. The only bright light in my life went out. Aunt Vera now was back to poverty and Cousin Delores was not much help at home. They both got jobs in a factory. Aunt Vera invited her boss home for dinner. She was trying to get enough money together to bury Uncle Jack, after his suicide. Low and behold, the funeral director fell in love with my beautiful Aunt, and buried Uncle Jack free, hoping that Aunt Vera would return his love. She did not feel the same and continued her dreary factory job.

Delores, my cousin, could just about maintain her job and through the kindness of their boss, they were both able to survive. Aunt Vera felt she was getting old and again, invited her boss home for dinner, hoping to fix him up with Delores, so she would be provided for. Again, another miracle. He fell in love with my aunt, and married her. Delores was a thorn in the marriage, but there was so much love that the marriage endured. The Angel of Death visited my beloved aunt and she died of cancer. My family lost track of Cousin Delores. Another chapter closing in my life with the loss of two dearly loved relatives.

A relative who passed briefly into my life was my Aunt Elsie. She was my mother's stepsister. After coming to this country from Ireland, she obtained a job in Shraft restaurant in New York City. While employed there, she met a charming con man. Enter Jack Descaines. They married and both were frequent visitors at my Uncle Harry's house. When Jack saw my Aunt May's many rings and diamonds, he decided to help himself to some rings. Uncle Harry pressed charges and Jack was incarcerated. This was a great secret but everyone knew about it.

Aunt Elsie then struck it rich and married an accountant. Alex Tardoff was a good catch. He didn't drink or smoke and made money. Every Monday night Al went bowling and this freed Aunt Elsie to kill some time and visit my mother. I looked forward to her visits because I was very hungry and she brought us some White Mountains rolls, which I devoured very quickly. Mama had been very poor; she really envied her stepsister. Can't blame her! Since we had nothing and no bright prospects to take us out of our poverty. Elsie envied my mother because she had two children and Elsie had none. My mother, feeling burdened with my sister and I, used to say, "What never made you laugh, will never make you cry." A dire prophesy to live up to. There is no feeling that can compare with not being wanted. Thus, low esteem.

SUNDAY OUTINGS

Sundays were spent visiting Calvary Cemetery. Aunt Ruth, Uncle Tommy, Uncle Harry, Mama, Daddy and I always went to the cemetery for our Sunday walk. It was there I learned Mathematics, hopping back and forth between the tombstones and figuring the birth date and the death date of each person. This outing was a little different than the outing children are normally taken on. At the end of the cemetery was a bar and grill. I loved the bar and grill because I could get pretzels and soda there. Also there was a spirit of happiness and singing. My Daddy had a great singing voice and every one would ask him to sing. He would look longingly at my Mama and sing, "Jeannie with the Light Brown Hair". Whether my mother was drunk or sober, my father adored her and made my sister and I respect her. My father was a gentleman, and never told an off color joke or cursed. He would always respect my mother and make excuses for her. He blamed my Uncle Harry for Mama's drunkenness. I knew in my heart of hearts that Daddy was a broken man. All his dreams went up in smoke. Mama's dreams of becoming a nurse also were put on hold. So here are two old people with the stigma of alcoholism and poverty with two children, as an additional burden. There was not much fun in life for them. I was a sickly child, prone to high fevers and nightmares. Both my parents carried a lot of baggage and wounds from their life. I believe they did their best with what they had and that's all we can do with the poker hand that is dealt to us in this vanishing city.

My Mama tried hard to be a good parent but God help her, she lacked the skills, due to the poor parenting in her own life. If we want to blame our parents, we must go into the past and dig up their parents. No fault insurance is the game we must play. Shame and blame only keep us in the prison of the past. When Jesus knocks on the door of our heart, it opens from the inside. Forgiveness is the key to the lock.

I was a very quiet introverted child and unable to speak what was in m yheart. Mama used to walk me to school, only about 5 blocks away from our home on 48th Street. She walked with a lady called Mrs. Marmin, who had one son, Harry, the class cut-up. Harry became a Supreme Court Judge. We wore the school uniform, brown dress with white collar and cuffs. She used to scrape up enough money to take me out to lunch at a little restaurant called Bennets. I suppose she got drunk after this, because I found her passed out and in a come. My poor sick mother suffered greatly from alcoholism and loneliness.

After my confirmation, I became deeply rooted in my faith. I used to ask a boy Jimmy Rogers, to go to daily Mass with me. All my younger years were spent trying to help people. I forgot that I was a "people" also. I felt it strange that my Mama and I went to confession weekly and Daddy never went to Mass, but again, we did not ask questions. I was told, "Be seen and not hears", so I became invisible. I turned my pain inside and I became an avid reader and an over achiever in school. I was never satisfied with anything less than an A+. I loved English and written composition. A schoolmate, Margaret Gornly, stole my composition and submitted it as her own. The nun, Sister Sienna, told her that she knew it was not her work buth minc. I never said a word or betrayed my schoolmate. This began a life long pattern of behavior, always remaining silent and not defending myself. The pain of my life twisted my emotions until I felt like I deserved to suffer. I met people and invited them into my life to fulfill my self-defeating prophecy.

I was an over achiever and tried hard to be an excellent student. I spent my childhood studying and no matter what mark I got, Mama would tell me I could do better. Perhaps this was good since it motivated me to please my mother and father. Because I was quiet and introverted, I did not play with anyone. My mother made excuses for me by saying, "Still water runs deep". After a while I gave up on trying to please my parents. Now I tried to get love from my father by play-acting. Mamas used to announce me like on the radio, as a singer and I used to sing and dance to get their attention. It worked for a little while. The loneliness I felt was as compared to Thomas Merton's book, "The Dark Night of the Soul".

17

On rare occasions after Mama prodded Daddy to pay attention to me, he would take me for a walk up to the empty lots on our block. While there, I would feed the birds. Daddy never spoke to me but I was so hungry for his love that even this silence was welcome. Mama always said, "Children should be seen and not heard", so I became invisible. These family secrets come back to haunt you later in life.

My playmates were much better adjusted than I was. I did not mix well, nor was I popular with the children my age. A neighbor, Mrs. Blanchard gave me a Princess Elizabeth doll for a Christmas gift. Mama said the only reason I got the doll was because of Mama's goodness to Mrs. Blanchard. I was only allowed to take the doll out of the box and then it was put away. I was not allowed to undress her or take her crown off. I never found out what became of the doll.

My sister, who came and went out of the house, I am not sure where she was. At this time she gave me a black kitten. Mama got rid of the little kitten. I worshipped my sister; She was my hero and my mother substitute. Despite her multiple personalities, when she was Mary Ellen, she was kind to me. Mama made her set my hair in rags, and she hated this chore, so she pulled my hair, but I never cried or told anyone. I didn't want to cause any trouble for her, so I suffered in silence. She used to like classical music and taught me about Beethoven on those rare moments when she was kind. Since there was 19 years difference between us, she was a mother figure to me. One day my sister told me I was the illegitimate child of a man called Dan Gallagher, from the local bar. I never spoke about this to anyone. In a way it explained my father's distant and cold attitude toward me. Again I turned the pain inside, but the wounded child turned to food to fill the empty hole in my soul.

CHIRSTMAS

I used to look forward to Christmas time. The nuns told us nice stories about the birth of Jesus. I believed Santa would come to my house and bring me presents. One Christmas, Daddy rented a Santa Claus suit and came through the back door shaking a bell. Mama asked him if he wanted a drink. Both picked up a drink. There were no presents because Mama said it was a Jewish holiday and the sales were better after Christmas. She never got to buy any of the sale items.

After while, I asked Mama if there really was a Santa Claus. This was the end of the Christmas tree and darkness descended on the house. No tree, no decorations, because it was a pagan holiday. I never had any toys so I became an avid reader. My favorite books were Nancy Drew mysteries. Birthdays came and went unnoticed. The message was, "You really didn't matter". I remember only one birthday party, but I can't recall if I got any presents.

Mealtimes were painful events. My sister was very tall and she used to tip the table when she sat down. Daddy yelled her and she ran into the back room and told me she was going to bleed to death. I always seemed to have to make a choice between people. There was no happiness in our house.

UNCLE HARRY

I have fond memories of my Uncle Harry teaching me math with matchsticks. He lived 4 blocks away from my Mother and Dad. He used to come and visit my mother and drink with her. Uncle Harry had more money; and a better job than my Dad did, so mother never missed an opportunity to compare them. My father was a waiter and my Uncle Harry was a plasterer who helped build Tammany Hall. Uncle Harry and Aunt May were very prosperous. They had 4 children. The oldest, Joan, became a nun—Sister Mary Henry. The next oldest was Cousin Harry, who studied to become a priest and then dropped out of the order. Then there was Clarie, who left home to marry a very rich man, and Arthur, the baby of the family, who became a cop and worked in Harlem.

When I was about 5 years old, Mama and I used to visit Uncle Harry. It was never an ordinary visit. Uncle Harry always had alcohol, and when my Mama could not afford to buy it, she visited her brother. He lived on the ground floor of a walk-up. There was a stoop and 4 steps leading into his apartment. Some bushes surrounded the stoop. Mama used to drink alone, and could not drink socially with Uncle Harry. She felt if no one sees you drink, you couldn't get drunk. Wrong! After a while, she would stagger home to Daddy and he blamed my uncle for Mama being drunk. Uncle Harry got sick and tired of being blamed and having his liquor depleted, so one day, he decided not to let us in.

Locked out, Mama picked me up to peek in his window that was visible from the stoop. I, being a good reporter, said "Yes, Mama, I see him." Mama wanted to make sure I was telling the truth. She climbed up on the steps and fell in the bushes. I kept saying, "Oh Mama!" I pulled her up out of the bushes. But she kept hitting me on the head with her pocketbook. I kept screaming for her to stop. Uncle Harry heard my screams, and we got in once again to his liquor—and Mama got drunk. Just another day!

My father needed to blame someone for Mama's condition, and so he blamed Uncle Harry and me! We had another tribal ritual on Sunday. My father's brother, Uncle Tommy and Aunt Ruth used to come to visit. We entertained them by visiting Calvary Cemetery. It was there that I learned math, hopping back and forth between the tombstones, figuring out the age of the dead. Gazing at tombstones, and picking flowers and ribbons from the graves was a real treat on Sunday. I never knew about zoos or pleasure trips.

Time went by on fleeted wings and I was getting older, but not wiser. My mother used to visit other—if you can call it that—on Sundays because of our own liquor shortage. Aunt May and her four children, Uncle Harry, Mama and I would sit in the dining room and Uncle Harry would put me on his knee. He kept his rosary in one hand and the other hand he put in my pants. Not sure at 5 years old what was happening, I was afraid to say anything for fear of hurting someone. This began a pattern of molestation. As a payment, he used to give me money to go to the movies. This was a treat, for we lived in poverty.

Uncle Harry never missed Mass. My father never went to church, but had Hell at home with Mama's alcoholism. Uncle Harry and Aunt May had a great life. Aunt May spent money as fast as Uncle brought it home. He used to ask her if she had a boyfriend or if she gambled. She did neither, just drank and spent money. The family was well fed while we were starving 4 blocks away.

One time I borrowed my cousin, Claire's pink angora sweater, and was wearing it when Aunt May saw me, and began shouting that I stole the sweater. I surrendered the sweater, but the hurt remained. She shamed me in front of my friends.

RUNNING AND RUNNING

I was now on the run from the Hell I lived in at home to Uncle Harry's house four blocks away. One bad scene ran into another. I never spoke of my Uncle Harry's molestation, or his son, the ex-priest because some how or other, I felt like I was to blame. I also did not want to hurt my mother or uncle by remembering these dark secrets. Sweep them under the rug. Pretend they never happened and maybe they will go away.

Another "run away" was four blocks away from my home to my sister's home. She used to let me sleep on the couch. One night, my brother-in-law, Alfred got up, loosed my blouse. Another secret! My sister kept asking me about it and again not wanting to hurt anyone, I kept silent and ran back home again.

GRADUATION FROM
ST. THERESA'S

I completed 8 long years in St. Theresa's school. Now it was time
to graduate. Our pastor, Father Manton, was known to have a severe
drinking problem. He used to walk his dog at night, and was seen
falling down. We don't talk about that. Father Manton gave out our
reports cards. He would enter the classroom with a red face and say.
"You are all promoted with the exception of; then with a long pause,
he would announce the one person left back. Poor Catherine Murphy,
6 foot tall, 18 years old, and we left her back. What an embarrassment
for her.

After report cards we lined up for the mass. Mass over, now Father
Manton gave out awards for exceptional students. I received the English
Medal and had no sooner sat down; when he called me up again to
get the religion and honor award. Mama said she was ashamed of me
because I took so long to get up to the altar to get the medals. Her
words will be forever in my heart and soul. Slow Motion! I was never
good enough no matter what I did or achieved. A classmate, Anne
Fahoney, complimented me. She later became a nun.

After our graduation, Mama decided to have a party for me. It
was another drunken orgy that my mother's relative and Dr. Dalinksy
attended. Looking back at the picture that was taken, I looked very
old. There was a basket of flowers, much like the ones you see beside a
casket, in my hands. And the party went on.

SCHOLARSHIP TO
BISHOP MCDONNELL

St. Theresa's school awarded 4 scholarships to be given to outstanding students. This prestigious award entitled the recipient to four years of free tuition. We were to be notified by mail in the hope that we won. Never dreaming I would win, but never the less I went to the mailbox daily in the hope that just maybe I would be selected.

One day, mother was out and she took her mailbox key with her. I did my daily trek and was a yellow card and tried to peek through the slot, but found it impossible to see all the words. I borrowed an eyebrow tweezer from Mrs. Powers, my mother's neighbor, and little by little, piece by piece, I extracted the card. What a joy to learn I won the scholarship. Mother and Dad would surely be proud of me. Wrong! When Mama came home and I showed her the card, she said, "I told you not to show emotion." She was angry with me for being so excited. I knew at that moment, I would never please her, no matter what I did. She was too sick. Daddy was not impressed! I believe I also shut down my emotions to become a non-person. Low Self esteem! No self esteem! Always looking for outside approval.

The long hot summer was spent, by being told that since there was no uniform at this school, Mama and Daddy could not afford my clothing.

SUMMER JOB

Since the summer was long and there was no money for the school that was coming up soon, I studied the ads in the paper for a job. I saw an ad for a job as a companion to a woman with multiple sclerosis. I looked much older than my age, so I applied for the job.

Henney Woerlein was an obese German woman who was partially paralyzed and in a wheelchair. She was raising her sister's child. My job was to lift her and feed her meals. Her brother-in-law lived in the apartment with them. He was an older man and he was attracted to me. He worked in a sweater factory and used to give me sweaters. I used to avoid him when he came from work. I was wounded by my uncle and cousin, and felt that no one could be trusted.

BISHOP MCDONNELL

School and Bishop McDonnell were a frustrating experience for me. The nuns were very cold and demanding. Being in school was just as bad as being at home.

The school was located in Jackson Heights. This required a 5-cent toll on the train. Most of my schoolmates were very well dressed and financially secure. Since I had no clothes except one blouse and skirt. I felt very out of place. I went to school with 10 cents and a skimpy sandwich. In order to get a coke at the local candy store, like the other students, I knew I would have to duck under the turnstile, and take my chances at being caught. It was worth the scare. I wanted to have things like my classmates.

Conditions at home reached an unbearable limit for me. Daddy still blamed me when Mama was drunk, which was most of the time. I had a great love for my mother and tried to protect her. I would search and search for her bottles and try to clean up her mess before my father came home. I am sure that she tried to stop drinking but always lost the battle. When she was sober she was very protective of me. She never let me out of her sight. She didn't want me to play with the other children. I used to sit at the living room window very lonely and lost.

One time my mother expressed a desire for a coffee table and a Persian coat. I saved up my baby-sitting money and kept putting a deposit on a coffee table at a local store, I was so excited when they delivered it. I guess I always tried to make her happy for my being born. Mama promptly took it back and got the money for it, saying it was an extravagance. I never got her the coat.

My mother never seemed to appreciate anything. Despite daily Mass and Communion, her depression spread its ugly tentacles throughout our home. I knew I was powerless over her addiction and her unhappiness. I withdrew into books and studies and had a good academic record.

When we were marched downstairs to attend Benediction there was no head count and I saw my chance to escape. I used to go to Rockaway Beach where there was music and dancing and laughter. I found a dance partner and danced and danced. The next day I hated to go to school. My friends were very well dressed and I felt like an orphan, which I really was. I not only felt different, I was different. My grades began to fall below my usual high standards. I was deteriorating in body and soul. My desire to achieve was gone and I played hooky every chance I got. In those days no one cared enough to question the decline in my work. It was only a matter of time before I dropped out of school, which was a great disappointment to Mama and Daddy. They said I broke their hearts, however, they had never recognized my accomplishments, only my failures.

My home was no home for me. I tried to take on the role of being my Mother's mother. I looked older than I was.

I tried to take a typing course at home, but failed. I really quit life but no one noticed or cared.

HOLIDAYS

My first Christmas at Bonwit Teller's was a gala affair. The sales girls were so generous; they gave me so many gifts that I could barely carry them home. For some reason, my home was a dark, sad place. They were always saving on electricity. We never had a Christmas tree, because they cost money. Mama had a small nativity stable in the living room where I slept. This was the only indication that it was a holiday.

Mother celebrated the holiday with a turkey dinner. The ordeal of cooking this turkey seemed to overwhelm my mother. No one saw her drink, but she was always staggering around the kitchen. She had a theory that, if no one saw her drink, she couldn't possibly get drunk.

We often ate very late on each holiday. Mama suffered from a disease, which I laughingly called Turkey-itus. She had severe attacks of self-pity, while the guests were waiting to be served. These anxiety attacks were accompanied by cursing all the relatives who pretended not to hear. If I close my eyes I can see my dearly beloved Mother sewing the turkey and mumbling about the ingratitude of the guests. One year I bought my Mother basting pins to alleviate the strain of this ordeal. She ran out of them and put her hatpin in for the final touch.

After Mama drank some more alcohol in secret, she put the turkey in the oven, but forgot to remove her mesh shopping bag. By this time, she was in a coma from the whole ordeal, while we waited and waited for our dinner. Everyone was seated and I can see then all now, Aunt Tommy and Uncle Ruth, appropriately named since Aunt Ruth was the boss, Uncle Harry with his rosary in his hands, Cousin Arthur, and my sister with her important boyfriend. Dad sat at the head of the table pretending everything was fine.

My cousin Arthur went into the kitchen to try to speed up the dinner since it was now 10:00 at night. Mother was sleeping and when Arthur opened the door to the oven, he saw the mesh shopping bag, which had gotten air into it and was vibrating. He said, "Oh, my God, the turkey is alive and moving." He saved the day and removed the shopping bag. At last dinner was served. Mama forgot to remove her hatpin, and my sister's boyfriend got the hatpin. He held it up and said, "Someone must have swallowed the hat!"

Daddy got very angry with him, not at my Mama. We were taught, never to disrespect my mother. I was always told to be seen and not heard, so I became invisible and never said a word.

Dinner, just another drunken orgy, was finally over, and the guests went home. My sister made a resolution to rent a family for the next celebration, since her romance ended with that boyfriend.

MISDIAGNOSIS OF
MY DISEASE

The long summer vacation was coming to an end, and I became very ill. The doctor who examined me was very cruel, and the cold speculum he used broke my hymen. Despite my screams he continued to keep me on the table in his office. He detected an infection and I was hospitalized. After another examination he discovered that I had a cyst, which he could not reach, so he cut a window in it and let it drain. He also discovered that I only had one kidney, the left kidney was missing. My poor mama was very upset and we rode home from the hospital in a taxicab. Mama drowned her sorrow in alcohol. She lived a lonely isolated life because my father was never home. His job as a waiter demanded him to work long hours and he received very little pay for his work. It is no wonder they both were very disillusioned and unhappy with their lives.

Time went on and I always felt like a misfit. No matter how hard I tried, my family considered me slow, in spite of an excellent academic record in school. They needed to vent their own failures on someone. I was "IT". Be seen, not heard, was drummed into my brain. I became invisible.

DR. BERGER'S OFFICE

Dr. Berger and his brother, a medical doctor, shared a rather elegant office on 5th Ave. I looked much older than my age so I applied for a job as a dental assistant for Dr. Berger. I was hired to assist the two doctors. The father lived in the back of this office and the housekeeper, Mrs. Corrigan, an old Irish lady, kept the offices clean and cooked for Dr. Berger. It was a cost effective arrangement.

The patients that came to the dental office were wealthy businessmen and mostly Jewish. My boss, Arthur, was a real character. He refereed wrestling matches as his hobby and gave me tickets to his wrestling matches. He made mouthpieces for fighters also. Once a week he closed his office for 2 hours and played cards with some of the businessmen. He married an ex-showgirl and had a home in Glen Cove, Long Island, to which he traveled daily.

He tried to teach me to take impressions but I was not really interested in being a hygienist. He did dental work for my Mother and I believe this is why he would not give me the raise I asked for.

Because everyone thought that I was older, I had dates with some of his friends. He introduced me to this brother Herbert, an officer in the Navy. I was too immature to appreciate the fine restaurants and elegance to which I was exposed. I was very unhappy at home at this time. I was constantly running away to my sister's house for short periods of time. My sister was very disturbed and her marriage was in jeopardy. She was very unhappy with her German husband and her life.

MRS. VARLET'S CANDY STORE

My mother always forbade me to go to a certain candy store. She said that bad people hung out there. My mother swore Mrs. Varlet was evil and rented upstairs rooms to the kids. I used to pass by and look inside. When I heard the music I was instantly drawn to the fun. Mrs. Varlet and her husband were from France. All the local jerks hung out there. They used to bring their liquor and spike the cokes. I am not sure Mrs. Varlet knew it. There was dancing and singing there and I went home to nothingness. A young girl, Joan Mc Kane, hung out there. She married Bobby Larson, an alcoholic who abused her. He used to beat-up on her. She was pregnant. I first saw my husband-to-be there. I fell instantly in love with him. I used to follow him and Joan Mc Kane down the street and hide in doorways so they couldn't see me. I think he was in love with her. One day he and Bobby got into a fight over her. It seems that Bobby beat Dick to the ground.

I had a crush on Dick and when he asked me to go out I gladly accepted. I was staying at my sister's house at the time. When Dick came to call for me, he had a hole in the knee of his pants and tried to cover it up. I assumed he had another losing battle with Bobby Larson. I had a crush on him and he took me to bars. I would never drink very much. His crowd was very fast. They were not like any people I had ever known. They used to fight and get drunk. He took me to a house party where the guests set fire to the curtains. It certainly seemed to me that they were all running around with each other's wives. I remember one boy, Tommy Robinson, who liked me. Once when he and Dick and I were in the bar, they went into the bathroom. When they came out dick said, "I'll never fight over you". The handwriting was on the wall.

This was a precursor of the life I would have with Dick. He was a very quiet depressed man just like my father. When he asked me to marry him, I felt he must ask my father. He came to my house. The fact of my one kidney was mentioned and my father said, "She's nothing but a hospital bill". Father asked if Dick had a job. Dick said that he would get one. My father said: "After you get the job come back and see me". Dick got a job in Willingbay's Camera Store in New York City. He made a very small salary but he was learning about photography. I wanted Dick to meet my boss, Dr. Berger. When Dr. Berger met Dick he asked him about his navy experience and concluded that he was a loser. He tried to introduce me to other patients but I was not used to being treated nicely so I continued to make wedding plans with Dick. My mother wanted a church wedding. I just wanted to get out of the house.

Another man that I truly loved was Bill Gustafson. He was a gentleman and on leave from the Marine Corps. He used to take me to a little bar in a cellar and have the piano player sing songs to me. I was not used to kindness and could not appreciate it, so I continued to see Dick.

My mother proceeded with the wedding plans. She was busy crossing names off her list and remarking on the cost of the wedding reception. It was to be small because Mama was the boss. I bought a green suit like I would wear to work. I had no desire to get married. Mama kept pushing for a date. Both Mama and Daddy came to City Hall to secure my license and sign away my life. They had to give their permission because I was very young. I can see them now in my memory.

WEDDING DAY

I knew, in my heart of hearts, that this marriage was not meant to be. Lo and Behold! The priest who married us was Father McCloud with whom I had shared my home problems. What a cruel joke. I wanted to run out of church that day. It was a quiet affair and I did not stay to greet the guests. Dick shook hands with everyone but I did not hang around. From the church we went to the Boulevard Restaurant. I felt very "out of it and lost". It was a sad affair. I could play pretend very well so I made believe that I was happy. We left and went to a dismal room on Lexington Avenue. We shared an apartment with an old man who had many prostitutes visit him. He claimed they were "his nieces". What a wonderful beginning for two newly weds. A raunchy dreary room in a dismal neighborhood. I had left one dark scene at home and traded it for another dark scene. I maintained my job with Dr. Berger. He gave me a nice wedding gift and all the patients gave me very nice gifts.

I was not happy living in one room and sharing the bathroom with the old man and his prostitutes. Mother suggested we live at her house. This meant sleeping on the floor. I had graduated from the love seat to the floor. Mother bought us a mattress but would not take the paper off it. You could hear our every move. This was a terrible arrangement for newlyweds. Mother did not want us there and it was obvious to everyone but me. I was so used to suffering that I did not know what a healthy situation was.

Mother suggested we apply for housing since she had lived in the metropolitan area for so many years. We did as directed. Mama was the boss.

FIRST APARTMENT

Our first apartment was on the second floor of the Metropolitan Apartment Project, just like where Mama lived. At last we had a bedroom of our own with a real bed. Dick was working in Willingbay's Camera Store and I was working in the Golden Rule, a family owned department store. One day as I was walking to work there was a car crash and I saw a little girl lying in the street. I was horrified to see a little girl, I had just seen alive playing, now dead in the street. My husband showed no emotion. This was to be a lifelong pattern of his indifference. Perhaps this lack of visible emotion started when his mother died. He told me that his mother died at home in Maine and he hid under the bed while the undertakers broke his mother's legs to carry her out. I am sure that this contributed to his indifference and inability to share emotion. We all carry baggage from our lives and we enter into relationships expecting other people to remove our baggage.

CREEDMOOR

Around this time, my sister had a child. I really loved this beautiful brown-eyed child. After her birth my sister had a nervous breakdown. She had to be taken out of her apartment in a straight jacket and in an ambulance. She was committed to Belleview Hospital for observation.

Then she was transferred to Creedmoor Hospital. I was in a state of shock, seeing my hero sister wild and fighting. I wanted to die or trade places with her. Creedmoor was a dreary sad—place; like a scene—from "One-flew Over The Cuckoo's Nest". The staff kept her in a zombie state with Thorazine. The patients were kept in slippers, and some were really psychotic, constantly fighting and arguing with each other, walking around talking to themselves. I felt such a deep sorrow seeing my sister, my hero, in the cell-like hospital. Mother was no support, she needed help herself. I saw my sister's psychiatrist, who had diagnosed her as a Schizophrenic. He felt she needed shock treatments.

I looked older than my age, and Mama couldn't face the truth about her other daughter, so I was elected to have a conference with her nurse, Mrs. Lynch, who, clearly did not like my sister. Whenever she acted out, they put her in a straight jacket. I went to see her weekly with her arms all black and blue, and she would accuse me of having an affair with her husband. This was not true, but she believed it to be true. She would order me to leave the hospital. Before leaving, I gave Mrs. Lynch $15.00 to take my sister out on the grounds. I also gave another nurse $10.00 to fix her hair. Both nurses always put her in a straight jacket before I bought her some kindness. My heart was broken seeing the insane state my role model was in. My brother-in-law, Captain Cordes, gave my niece, Maryellen, to my mother to care for. When I tried to visit my little niece, my mother would not let me I, stating that she was bathing the baby.

Christmas came and my sister was still in Creedmoor, now she was getting regular shock treatments. Every time I visited, she looked like a zombie, but was very quiet. She had to appear before the Lunacy Board that had committed her, before she could be released. They kept declaring her of unsound mind. Finally she was allowed to go home for the weekends. On one of these home visits, she became pregnant. My niece Debbie was then born.

MARRIAGE WAS OVER

My marriage was over now. I had thrown God out of my life, and neither my husband nor I went to church. This was the beginning of my decent into Hell. My husband constantly invited his evil friends to our house. Most of them were alcoholics and sociopaths. They used to drink and tell tales of their lives.

Betty and Phil were a couple that my husband knew from his school years. Betty was having extra-marital affairs, while Phil was working at night. She used to ask me to go out with her to the bars. On one of our nights out, she met my old boyfriend, and she slipped him my phone number. He called. And we met for a date for the movies.

Arguments then began at home over trivial things like my cat. I would run away to Betty's place or my sick sister's house, who only recently had been released from Creedmoor Hospital. I was essentially homeless, but didn't know it at the time.

I had another evil friend, Margie, who took me to a bar and we had pizza. Her husband, Danny was in jail, and she had four children at home with her mother. Feeling sorry for, I became her best friend, despite the fact that she was twenty years my senior. While we were at this bar, she met a man who had been in jail with her husband, Danny. He gave her some money for the children. He seemed like a nice friendly man and he offered us a ride home. He dropped her off at her house first, then sped off to a deserted spot; took out his gun, tore off my clothing, and raped me repeatedly. I tried and tried to scream, but he then told me that he was a two-time loser. He said that he might as well kill me before going back to jail again. I begged him to take me to my sister's house and promised he could spend the night with me. God must have been with me, even though I had abandoned

Him at that moment. The man believed me and drove me to my sister's apartment. She lived in a place where there was a security guard on duty. I struggled and ran out of his car and into my sister's apartment. She pulled me inside and the man sped away.

My sister blamed the whole incident on my friend Margie, and swore that she had sold me. I blamed myself. Once again my low self-esteem surfaced. My husband still lived in our apartment. He now had a roommate name Arthur B. Another low-life who physically abused his mother, and apparently she threw him out. I ran back to my husband and told him that I had been raped. Again he showed no emotion or compassion, so I left him with his friend, Arthur, and went home to Mama, who didn't want me either. My father had his foot bandaged and when I asked him what had happened, he said he had a dream that he was kicking a cat, but kicked the wall and broke his foot. My mother told me that my husband had beaten him up. Another family secret. My father was always a gentleman and didn't want to hurt me.

I'm sure I was having a nervous breakdown at this time. My sister's illness really scared me, being homeless, and my failed marriage was very painful. I had no one to confide in, or nowhere left to run. I remembered being told, "children are to be seen and not heard". So I became invisible.

Dick gave up our apartment, sold all the furniture I had worked so hard to acquire, and took off to California. Bill, my friend, was going away to be stationed somewhere, and I was alone and lost. One night before he left, we were walking down the street, and I saw my furniture in Packing Storage, with a "For Sale" sign on it. I ran back to my sister's house. She and Capt. Corbes, her husband, and two children were getting ready to go to Alabama, where he was stationed. The journey to a small town so far away was a long one and very emotionally charged. My brother-in-law had sent money home so my sister would learn to drive. He stopped the car, thinking she had taken lessons, and when she got behind the wheel, she didn't know what to do. This caused some chaos, but we proceeded to Alabama. My brother-in-law was very thrifty. We rented one room and everyone was packed into this small room to save money.

I called Bill, and he offered to take me to Pensacola Florida, where he was stationed. My sister and brother-in-law were happy to see me go. Bill was just about the most respectful man I had ever met. He never tried to get fresh with me. After being brutally raped, this came as a surprise to me. I believe he wanted to marry me, but I can't recall why we didn't. I tried to get a job in Pensacola to pay for my rented room, but I never succeeded, so finally I went home to the nothingness of my life. And once again "There Was No Room at the Inn", so I went from Uncle Harry's house to Betty's couch.

BLUE HAVEN

Betty used to take me to a bar in Elmhurst called the Blue Haven. It became the Devil Haven for many patrons. My sister's husband was away at the time, so she used to go there with us. I was very pretty back then and had very long blonde hair. I used to attract men and they used to buy my sister and I drinks. It was there in this sordid place that she met her present husband. He was very handsome and had a job as a police officer. This is what she was looking for, a steady salary and a way not to work. She was receiving $300 a month for her two children from Captain Corbes. I'm wondering how sick she was, or was she really slick and smart?

Time went on and I got a job at the White Castle as a carhop. It was there that we would drink vodka and orange juice.

Betty and I still did the bar scenes together. She was going with a gangster at this time. I met a tall handsome truck driver and we dated until Betty's mother found out that he was married.

My father then found out about the married man, and at my mother's insistence, he began beating up on me. I left home after that and I rented a room in Mt. Vernon. There was an Italian girl living there who brought me food from her mother's house. I was broke and lost. It seems like my friend Tom's son got sick and he went back to his wife. Another loss!

I ran to my sister's house to borrow some money. She hid me in the bedroom because she did not want her boyfriend to see me. She threw $20 at me and I left.

I had no life and nowhere else to run. My mother suggested that I go to California and pick up my dysfunctional marriage. She gave me $200 to go on the train and get out of her life. I took the train from Grand Central and Dick met me in California. He took me to a bar, as usual, and introduced me to two of his friends. It was instant dislike on their part for me. I never saw them again after that initial meeting. Because of my feelings of low self-esteem, I assumed there was something wrong with me.

He then introduced me to another weird friend, called Drew, who told me that my husband had been having a great time, with a lot of women, until I came. So you see, he was not waiting for me with baited breath.

We rented an apartment in a private house and I tried to be a housewife and a cook. I tried to take on a mother role for Dick, since he had told me of his mother's tragic death when he was 12 years old. I saw very little of California, as we were always out of money. I secured a job in a hosiery shop. The man hired me because at another time I had worked for his brother in New York.

I met a lady there called Ray, who seemed to be having a lot of fun. She was a heavy drinker, and invited me to see a famous piano player, who was appearing in a local bar. I really felt like I was missing out on life. I was very young and did not do the things that other young people did. I had missed a lot of my life. There was no high school graduation and no prom for me. I seemed to go from one bad situation to another. I felt no happiness in this marriage, but I was determined to make it work. My low self-esteem spoke loudly to me, telling me there was something wrong with me. Thus, the title of my story, "A Room Without Roaches, PLEASE."

I was so lonely in this dysfunctional marriage that eventually I went to the Shelter, and got two dogs to fill the emptiness of my life.

We moved out of the apartment and I met an older lady who was renting the top half of one of her houses. She was delighted to rent to me, with my two dogs. Mrs. Webb was a dog lover, who had twenty dogs she had adopted. She sat the dogs at her big dining room table, and they all ate together. One dog was her favorite, a mischievous mutt she called Dimple Darling. Her husband had been a famous editor for the Los Angeles Examiner, and I assume he had left her well off, so she was able to indulge her hobby of taking in strays.

My silent husband was neither for nor against my adoption of the two dogs. One I named Rough Stuff, and the other was called Cookie. They were very wild, but good company, and they filled a void that I felt in my marriage to my ever-silent husband.

Meanwhile, my mother kept writing to me with sad tales about my sister's behavior. Mama always excused her favorite daughter's behavior by saying "She's sick and doesn't mean it." No matter what mean thing she did, I was taught to overlook it. Grin and bear it.

Mother wanted me to come home. I also found out I was pregnant. My neighbor, Viola, was delighted and invited me to sew some clothing for our little Tom Tinker, as she named him. When Mama learned of the baby, she sent me a letter reminding me that I only had one kidney, and the doctor back home knew my condition, and perhaps would die in California.

As I mentioned earlier, Mama was the boss, so we made plans to go back home. No money as usual. I'm not quite sure what Dick did with his pay, and I never felt good enough, or worthy enough to ask. This was the beginning of a long line of silent abuse that I suffered in my marriage. Today when we apply a diagnosis to this type of silent abuse, in children, it's called "Failure to Thrive Syndrome". I received a steady injection of silent abuse throughout all the years of my marriage.

Since we had no money, my landlady, Mrs. Webb, advanced me $300 to go back home. I promised to repay her when we returned to New York. We had an old car, and we set off for home, because Mama was the boss.

Dick got an eye infection while driving through the Mohave Desert in Arizona. He was silent and angry. We stopped over at a motel and barely spoke to each other. There was no love, or affection, or joy at my having our first child. In his attitude towards me. The ride through the desert was long, hot, and silent.

We finally arrived at my mother's house. After all her letters urging me to return home, we were not welcome. Most especially with the dogs and so little money. Dick didn't have a job or the energy to look for one. I got the help wanted ads from the paper, and he saw a job at Republic Aircraft. In order to support him, I rode out to Long Island and sat for several hours in the car, pregnant, to wait for him. He finally came out and and told me he was hired. I guess the only thing he qualified for was a menial job, sorting airplane parts.

We drove home to Mom and Dad with the good news, and I overheard a conversation with Mother saying she wondered when we were leaving. My Dad was very silent about it, just like Dick, he did not want to respond.

When I tearfully asked him if it were true that they wanted us to leave, he neither denied nor affirmed it. I knew then that I had married my father, silent and withdrawn. I was always looking for love in all the wrong places, and with people that had none to give, and thinking I could change things. Today I know, that this is a lonely search, which ends up nowhere. Like searching for water in a desert. However, back then, I deluded myself and forgave everyone but myself. I was programmed to turn the other cheek.

The broken heart is a lonely hunter. I sought outside things to fill the lonely hole in my soul. I was always the one who had to take the lead and find an apartment. My husband didn't seem to care about anything or anyone. As I previously stated, he was alienated from himself. I was about six months pregnant, and at Mother's suggestion, I finally got a physical from Dr. Schnell, an obstetrician who had treated me when I was a child.

Dr. Schnell used to introduce me as Miss Gallagher. He just couldn't get used to my married name, Howells. I was very big and pregnant and this became an office joke.

ROCKAWAY BEACH

I saw a furnished room for rent in the newspaper at Rockaway Beach. My mother made it clear that we were no longer welcome at her small apartment. The beach was a nice memory for me, since I used to love to dance there. However, the music stopped for me the day I got married.

The Irish lady that rented to us used to visit me in my room, while Dick was working. She saw there was very little food in my refrigerator. I'm sure that because of a lack of nourishing food, my little son, Ricky, suffered from poor nutrition. In those days very little was known about nutrition. Since I had very little education about food and motherhood, I did the best I could with little experience or knowledge.

I used to experience a terrible loneliness, since my husband was emotionally unavailable. I walked to the ocean, with my dogs. They were my only companions.

Back home to Mom's again, I was very pregnant, depressed and homeless. Again my husband looked to me to find housing for my family, soon to be. Mama let us stay there while I searched for another place to live. I found an apartment in Blissville that was so cheap it was unbelievable. The rent was very affordable, but the area was a smoke filled, dark factory district. The landlord accepted me and we moved in with no furniture, until I saw a couch for $20. Dick put the used couch on the top of his car with a twin bed, purchased from a wealthy lady in Forest Hills. It was in the sordid apartment that I awaited the birth of my first child. We needed a refrigerator since there was none in the house. I had to keep our little bit of food on the windowsill. We shared the bathroom with a little old drunken man who was always asleep on the toilet. The surrounding areas were dark, and since it was a factory district, there was a heavy smog. But not nearly as heavy as my heart. My depression was only heightened by my husband's indifference to me. There was no happiness in the union. Since I was programmed to believe that this was a Catholic Marriage and in those days, once a marriage was consummated, it could not be annulled, I tried to make the best of it. I was very young and hopeful, thinking I could change my husband and make him love me.

No one came to visit me in these surroundings. They were all living well and had enough money and nice apartments. I suppose my poverty was depressing to them. I had no close friends any more, and lived in isolation, waiting for my child to be born. It was a very painful time in my life. A time when other girls my age were roller-skating and dancing and doing teen age things. I had sold my soul for room and board, and thrown God out of my life.

RICKY'S BIRTH

My labor pains stated and we went to the hospital on Fifth Avenue, where my doctor practiced. I was heavily sedated and when I awoke they told me I had a little boy, five pounds and four ounces. They did not bring him to me because he was so small. When they finally did bring him to me, I saw a little blonde haired baby. He was so small, I was afraid of him. I held him very carefully, afraid he would break. He had blonde hair and looked like a little angel.

Mama felt that to bring him home to the cold water flat in the winter would be very dangerous to his health. So she decided, since she was the boss, that she would keep him with her in her nice cozy apartment, but not me or his father as there was no room for us. So we went to the cold water flat and I returned to Mama's daily to feed my baby.

Most of Mama's neighbors came to see him and to bring him gifts. I could not live without my baby, so I took him to the dingy place where I lived. I had no money for formula, nor a place to keep things cold, except for the windowsill outside.

One day my sister came to visit, when I had no formula for him. She said "Give him water". Then she quoted a story about my Aunt Mary giving her kids water. Dick finally came home and we got a can of evaporated milk for him. I was heart-broken because this was the first-born grandchild and they all had the money to buy him the things he needed. We didn't even have the money for a baby carriage. My mother told me of the great bargain she got, buying a shabby second hand carriage for ten dollars.

Do you wonder why I had such low self-esteem? I was so grateful for any small kindness that anyone showed me. The message was loud

47

and clear, that if anything was to be done about my poverty, I better do it. And I did! I got a job in a Q-Tips factory, and began working all night. I was so clumsy they kept moving me from one machine to the next. The factory girls were very negative and crude. They told off color jokes that I didn't understand because I was much younger than they were.

I didn't last there long. I made a little money, and took my new baby in his shabby carriage to the nearest store to buy him a little outfit. My silent husband didn't seem to care or to make any effort to improve our conditions. I know now how sick he was. His sister, Eva made drapes for our dingy apartment. She bragged about the bargain she had gotten, only twenty-five cents a yard. She meant well, but I felt ashamed when I heard she had come to our place while I was in the hospital. She was appalled at our living conditions. She had married a postman and was living in Greenpoint in a really nice place they had recently purchased. I was always jealous of my sister-in-law, she seemed to have it made. She was one of the twins, Eva and Edith, who where both in the army. Edith married a butcher who provided well for her. I felt like a beggar, looking into all these people's lives. They had made better choices than I, and were now reaping the rewards.

Now it was up to me, since I had no loving support from family or my husband, to get us out of this poverty. I used to walk the streets with my baby thinking of how I could make life better for him. I was alone and lost with my first-born son.

WHITE CASTLE

One day I saw a job offering for a carhop in the White Castle. The White Castle was a hamburger haven for poor people. I was hired to work at night at Elmwood. My hours were from 12:00 midnight until 7:00 A.M. We had to work outside, in the rain and snow, and run up to the cars to take their order. Mother agreed to mind baby Ricky at this time. I was making enough now to provide for my family, since Dick took no responsibility for my son or me. This was his life long pattern of alienation. I always made excuses for him, thinking I was the bad one.

Now we started drinking vodka and orange juice to keep warm. My friend Shirley and I had similar stories of abandonment, which we shared at night. My sister came to the White Castle one night and threatened me and told me my mother would not baby sit for me any more. I knew I needed to work, to find some kind of housing for us. One of my coworkers offered to help me. For $25 a week she and her husband, Whitey, said they would baby sit so I could go to work and save for an apartment that was decent for my family. I used to visit my tiny son and bring pampers for the baby sitters. One day I went there and her husband was bathing with my baby in the tub. I removed my child and quit my job. I had some money saved, and met a girl I once knew. I offered her father-in-law, the superintendent of a family house, a hundred dollars if I could have the first apartment. Money talks, and every one else walks. I got the apartment for a hundred dollars a month. No furniture, no money, with no outside help.

Dick now had a job with Good Humor selling ice cream, riding a bike all over town. If he made any money, I never saw any of it.

Again, I knew I had to do something to provide for my son, Ricky. A girl I knew, Joan S., had two illegitimate sons, and her mother and father took her in and gave their grandchildren any luxuries. She gave me a crib and clothing for my son. What a difference in families! One has to do with the person's ability to love. I came from an unloving family. I married a man who was incapable of loving anyone. I never thought I deserved anything better.

So here we are again, not enough money for food, or any of the necessities of life that people take for granted. We changed our address but did not change the poverty-ridden life or the dependency my husband had on me to always fix things. My role in life did not change. I became my silent husband's mother.

My son was very colicky. I took him to the doctor to get him an appetite stimulant to get him to eat. I used to visit my mother who lived across the street in her comfortable apartment. I was very close to my family. Ricky used to sit outside Mom's window in his second hand carriage, which I was ashamed of, and I sat with my mother crocheting. She made fun of me and was verbally abusive. I never remember any kindness or comfort with her. She said I don't like to cook. When Daddy came home, she gave him a cup of borscht. He ate most times at work. He was a waiter in the New York Stock Exchange.

I'm sure he traded his dreams, as an opera singer, for a way to survive. As he leaned over each table, no one saw the song in his heart, or cared. Mama used to buy him a small pint of ice cream, and none for me. I have had a craving for sweets for most of my life. I think I had a heart's desire to have some sweetness in my life.

My parent came to this life with very heavy baggage, which was compounded by their addiction to alcohol. I have learned to realize that they did the best they could with their poker hand. My sister took a flight into insanity, and was diagnosed Schizophrenic. She tried to create a new reality in a crazy atmosphere. She paid the price by being institutionalized in Creedmoor and Belleview.

My apartment was very bare and depressing. I remember I wall papered one wall with a rose colored paper in an attempt to brighten the place. We didn't even have a table to sit at until someone donated a table and four chairs. The one thing that I had that I treasured was my small blonde haired son. My husband was a shadowy creature who never paid attention to my son and I. I looked for love in my family and my husband, but they were incapable of loving themselves or me. I had a neighbor, Cooky, who had a loving husband and several children. They did things together and were very happy. Her husband was a hard workingman who did construction work.

Downstairs there lived another couple that were related to my friend, Cooky. Again I saw happiness but it eluded me. My dad used to visit me and we played cards and I forced myself to drink beer to be close to him. Uncle Harry, his friend Scotty, and Dad and I used to play poker. I adored my father and tried to be close to him. All the social life centered in my house although I was the poorest of the clan.

MY FATHER'S DEATH

It was the day after Christmas. My mother spent Christmas with my sister. Dad came to my house with my Uncle Harry. Christmas was over and Mom and Dad came to visit. Daddy complained of chest pains. He hated doctors and did not trust them. I inherited this trait from him. I gently suggested that Mama would baby sit and Dad and I would visit my doctor, who had treated my baby and I. Dad reluctantly agreed. Mama was drunk, and my husband was somewhere, not sure where. Daddy and I walked down to Dr. Elba, and I went in ahead of him to explain to the doctor my father's fear and he understood. When I went outside to the waiting room to speak to my father before his examination, he said, "The Hands of Time have wound out for me." I tried to change his mind by reminding him of all the victims in the hospital that really were dying. I didn't realize that he was dying and even more than that, he wanted to die. Dr. Elba gave him a prescription for hardening of the arteries and a clean bill of health. My Dad and I walked to the drugstore and filled the prescription. I assured him that he was going to be all right. I know now that he knew he was going to die.

When I got back to my apartment, my mother was drunk and sitting on the floor. She and my baby son were trying to ride a bicycle. Dad just looked at her, and as they descended the stairs to go home, my father said, "Please take care of your mother for me." I promised that I would. These were the last words I heard from my father.

I tried to sleep, but at 11:00, Dec. 26, my mother came pounding on my door, telling me that something had happened to my father. I ran out after her, and saw my beloved father lying half across a chair in their living room. I wanted to die instead of him. My mother kept drying and screaming that she had lost her best friend. Truer words were never spoken.

I never saw anyone die before, and I was so shocked I kept breathing into his mouth, happy to give him my breath of life. His eyes were wide open, as if he was staring, and his color was bad. Mother kept crying and then my sister and her new boyfriend came to visit. When she saw my father she too kept screaming.

I went to the phone and called the doctor that just a few hours ago had said that he was in good health. I now remembered my dad's last words to me "The hands of time have run out for me." Dr. Elba signed the death certificate and I asked him how this happened. He would not explain.

However, I went into the bedroom and I saw an old duffle bag belonging to my father, it was as if he was planning to leave. I'm not sure what happened on his final moment, but I do know he lived a life of hopelessness and desperation, with my mother's alcoholism. All his dreams went up in smoke.

I saw the television I had bought them turned on. I'm happy that I was able to provide some happiness for him, while he was here. I visited daily and he was always watching cowboys and Indians on the television. My regret is that I was always seeking my mother, and not paying much attention to him, although I loved him very much, he never showed much love for me, and when I married Dick, I was searching for a father. All I got was indifference since I was comfortable with the pain.

The next chore left for me to do was call the priest. The first question he asked was, "Did your father go to church?" I answered honestly, that he did not go to church. When the priest finally arrived to give the last rites, my mother and my sister told him I was mistaken, that he did go to Mass. In those days, if you did not go to church, you could not be buried with a Mass or have a Catholic funeral. Uncle Harry came while all this commotion was going on, and he and Mama had some drinks, with lots of excitement and drinking. I have memories of Uncle Harry, with his warped sense of humor, calling my father "Anti Christ". Another memory emerged of my Dad sitting outside Uncle Harry's house, and Uncle Harry setting fire to a newspaper (to imitate hell) and putting it under my Dad's chair. My father jumped up and almost had a heart attack on the spot! This was the uncle who molested me, but he never missed Mass on Sundays. What a mixed message that was! "Do as I say, not as I do". Uncle Harry had a good life, but my Dad lived in hell.

FATHER'S FUNERAL

I think Mama had an insurance policy with enough money for a decent burial. In those days the insurance man came weekly and sold a policy for twenty-five cents a week.

My mother and my sister showed up in mink coats, while I sat back and cried and cried. My Dad had been a great singer at parties, and one of his drunken friends came in and kept telling him to get up and sing a song. My sister kept showing everyone her diamond engagement ring. It appears that Otto, the cop, and she had gotten engaged. I could not even greet the family, I was so bereaved and sick. I wore a big orange coat someone gave me and I felt completely out of place. This went on for three days. I went home and slept in the coat. My silent husband was somewhere in the picture. I sat numb as my father was carried into the church that he never attended. But to my mother's satisfaction, he had a Catholic Mass.

After the burial, they all came back to my house. I supplied the food and the liquor, even though I was very poor. I wondered if my father would look down on the scene, and if he would approve. I was truly heartbroken, and I felt I was having a nervous breakdown. My son, Ricky, had just taken his first steps and my Dad lived to see that.

Mama and my sister decided to send thank you cards to the people who sent flowers. This was done in my house because they were fond of my shrimp salad. They did not put my name on the cards. My sister said that no one would know me. I never questioned their decision not to include me. This was a pattern that followed me all my life. I was always on the outside looking in. Mother's eyes were failing, probably due to diabetes and her vision was poor.

I was so afraid she would get run over, I used to follow her to church. Whenever I tried to take her arm, she would push me away and get angry. But despite her attitude, I persisted in walking her to Church. My husband used to say, "Your mother will be alright, but you'll get run over." I sincerely tried to help my mother through her grief over my father's death.

I had some money saved and I withdrew all my savings, about $300, and paid my mother's rent. Her rent was very low, and she constantly complained about not having enough money.

One day a lady from welfare came to my poorly furnished apartment and said my sister applied for welfare for my mother. She said my sister signed the document and she needed my signature also. Remembering my promise to my father, to take care of my mother, I was sure he would not have liked to have my mother on welfare. I told the social worker of my promise, and added that if my sister would contribute we would eliminate the need for my mother to be on "the dole". I also told her I would go to work to help her, besides having paid her rent. The social worker then informed me that it would go through, with or without me. I now knew that the only way I could keep my promise was to go to work.

How I would get a job, and how my small son would be cared for were problems to be solved. My husband offered no solution. He was not supportive and was emotionally removed from me and my son. I was breaking down under the cross I carried. I needed to get night hours close to home. Dick was working days at the time. Searching my memory back in time, I can't remember where he was working. I only remember dire poverty and very little furniture or food.

Mama was drinking very heavily now and I was afraid I would lose her too. I decided to take her away for a few days to Rockaway Beach, just to help her and to enjoy a change of scenery. There was no thought of myself, as there wasn't a self.

When I went to pick her up, she was drunk, and would not open the door. We had to call the superintendent to take the door down, because we feared Mama had joined my father. I was hysterically happy when we picked her up and got her into the car.

Finally arriving at Rockaway Beach to a furnished room on 98th Street, we to bed, and were soon awakened by a loud crash. Mama had somehow found some beer, and after drinking it, she had thrown the cans outside the door. I'm sure half the tenants heard the crash and knew what room it came from.

On the humorous side of this vacation, Mama used to steal things from the clothesline. One day she stole some socks and gave them to my husband to wear. My husband was talking to a neighbor and put his foot on the rail, and our neighbor said "By God, those are the socks I was looking for!" Embarrassing moments, but a funny story to recall.

We went home, Mama to her apartment across the street from me. I felt that I should keep my promise to my father to take care of my mother, although we were living in poverty ourselves. My husband had no answers or solutions. He barely spoke to me at all. My father's death had been a terrible loss to me. I really never got to know him in life. I know my mother needed money while waiting for her welfare, that I refused to sign for.

JOB AT O'CONNELL'S

Again I was called on to solve my mother's dilemma. Seeing a job in the local paper for a waitress, I applied. I was so depressed and heart-broken, that I just knew I needed money. The darkened bar was the only job I felt I was worthy of.

The old man was a heart-broken man, who had two sons, one was a criminal the other a singer and bartender in this dismal place. There was no food to serve but it was a bar and grill. I didn't know a thing about drinks, and when they asked me to tap a beer keg, I didn't know how to do it. The few people who came in tipped me but there was no salary. The bar had been a really lively place with D.A. and lawyers who came and spent freely. Then the owner's son was involved in a robbery, and he was sent to jail. My cousin was a dirty cop who acted as a look out. They all went to jail and while waiting for sentencing the D.A. and lawyers who used to come there stopped coming and the place was under surveillance. I never knew about the robbery. I never received a salary for my work. I knew I needed money for my mother. The owner of the bar was a close friend of my cousin, the dirty cop look out, and he threatened me not to ask for money or else. They told me to drink with the few customers they had left, and to drink only scotch, short drinks, so the bar could make money.

John O' came out of jail and introduced me to Chivas Regal Scotch. I quickly became addicted. I had always resolved never to look like my mother. I was becoming much worse! He was a violent criminal and introduced me to the racetrack. I never knew about racing before. He and his fellow criminals used to give me money to bet; since they were hot guys. I still know very little about racing or horses or tending bar.

After working for a while with no salary, I decided to try to get my job back at the White Castle. I truly wanted to help my mother despite the fact that she would not baby sit or help me in any way. My promise to my father kept whirring in my head. My mother baby-sat for my sister, explaining that she was very sick. She was really slick and devious. I was the one that was sick and in poor health operating with one kidney and a broken heart.

My husband was a shadowy figure, who had no identity with him. He never made enough money to live on, and I always made excuses for him.

BARBARA'S BIRTH

About six months after my father's death, I discovered I was pregnant. The White Castle had re-hired me but to work in Brooklyn. In those days the train was safe, but there were bar fights on the parking lot. I worked in the snow and rain, every night until early morning. At the end of the shift we had to sweep up the parking lot and put the garbage in bags. I worked with two girls, Ella and Francis, they were sisters. Both had help at home, so they could sleep. We drank vodka and orange juice to keep warm.

When fights broke out after the bars closed, we had to lock ourselves in the curb house to avoid being beat up. They gave us our tips in a bag. We did about twenty-five dollars a night. More money than my husband made. I couldn't wait until the next day to buy my son any toy he wanted. One toy he liked was Big Din, little monkey men. I barely got any sleep since my mother was baby sitting for my sister, who finally went to work in a factory. She didn't need the money because she was collecting $200 a month from Capt. Cordes, whom she refused to divorce. My two nieces, Mary Ellen and Debbie, were left alone while my sister ran around with Otto, the cop. One day mother came to visit and I had my tips from the night before, after working all night. My son, his grandmother, and I walked through the 5 & 10-cent store, and my baby was just starting to walk, he saw a toy he wanted and threw himself on the floor. While I was looking for money, my mother pinched him, and said her usual, "Good boys get everything, Bad boys get nothing." She never spent a nickel on my son. We didn't expect anything because she didn't celebrate Christmas or birthdays. Thus the title of my book, "A Room Without Roaches, PLEASE!" I did not have low self-esteem, I had no self-esteem!

Working in Brooklyn and not getting enough sleep was taking it's toll on me. My boss finally transferred me to Sunnyside, Long Island, which was within walking distance of my home. This was a great burden lifted, but I still did not get any sleep. Ricky was walking now and very active. I adored my blond little son.

After my father's death, I was in shock for a long time. Working long hours with no sleep made me high risk for any cold or measles going around. I worked with a red haired girl, a former hatcheck girl at the Copa Cabana, whose name was Carmen. She struck it lucky and met a drummer, and they planned to marry.

Carmen had no children, so she could sleep all day and come to work full of pep.

Around this time I went to the doctor who had delivered my son, and he found out that I was pregnant again. I had no prenatal care since I was so out of it mentally. I was surprised to learn that I was six months pregnant. Dr. Schnall reprimanded me for not taking better care of myself! How could I? I was working until seven in the morning, in sleet and snow, never getting any sleep.

My boss let me work, knowing I needed the money for my children. Customers who knew me, were afraid my baby would be born on a tray. I worked almost until my Barbara Jean was born. I never had a thought for myself, only for my mother and her grief.

When the circus came to town, I bought tickets for my mother and Uncle Harry with my tip money. They seemed to enjoy it. I was always trying to buy love. What a waste of time!

My labor pains started and I was afraid of doctors and hospitals, so I waited until the last minute to go to the hospital on 5th Avenue and 105 Street.

We took a cab, and I insisted on going to confession before we went. In the confessional I told the priest I was in labor. He gave me the absolution, and got rid of me fast. Meanwhile, the cab driver was telling me that if I gave birth in his cab he would have to sterilize his cab. My silent withdrawn husband said nothing as usual.

My daughter, Barbara Jean was born, without any painkillers, because I got there too late. She was a tiny baby, only five pounds, so they put her in an incubator. She was so small and fragile I was afraid she would break. My uncle promised to buy me a baby carriage if I had a girl. He kept his promise and Barbara had a brand new baby carriage. Now I had two children and very little money.

One day my friend Carmen came to see my baby and she saw the poverty and sparseness of furniture, she told me I could get my job back. This seemed to be the only thing to do, to get enough food and other things for my children.

Barbara Jean was a beautiful baby but very frail and delicate. I bought her a beautiful red dress in a child's specialty shop with my tip money. I used to take Barbara and Ricky in the brand new carriage to my sister's house and sit outside with them.

My Uncle Harry's house was another place I would visit with my two children. We sat on the stoop and neighbors would come and join us. One neighbor, Bessy Bender, appropriately named, was the most pitiful sight. A man named Scotty Heinz, fell in love with my lovely mother, and proposed to her.

Barbara was a very quiet child and Ricky was very aggressive. Working all night in the White Castle and getting very little sleep, gave me only a short time with my two beloved children. I had a friend, Kitty Kelly, who told me that I was missing my children's lives by working. She had about seven children and was madly in love with her husband.

I was so happy to have some money for clothing and food for my two children. I'm not sure what Dick did with his money, but we were always in poverty. My only regret was that my father did not live to see my tiny daughter, Barbara, in her pretty red dress.

My Uncle Harry, offered to baby sit at night, since Dick and I worked at night. I trusted him despite the fact that he had molested me. My daughter always had suspicious diaper rash and was always very inflamed around her vagina. She cried a lot. I tried to put Desitin on her, but nothing seemed to help her rashes. Barbara was a beautiful little girl and I loved her dearly.

Because I was working all night, at 7:00 in the morning, I used to put Ricky and Barbara in their playpen to try to get some sleep. Ricky was very playful and used to tease Barbara. She was a tiny, frail child. I never had enough time with my children because I had to work all night. I used to take walks in the daytime with my two children in their new carriage.

One day I heard an uncle was coming from Ireland to visit my Aunt Mary, who lived about twenty blocks from my house. After the long walk, I wanted to see my uncle, but I was not invited into the house. Another subtle put down to show that I didn't count! I was desperately unhappy in my marriage but since it was a Catholic marriage, I tried to make it work! My two children gave me a reason to live. I worked very hard, as a carhop, to provide for them, the only way I knew, I had dropped out of school to get married and had no skills or education. I was truly a lost soul.

MOTHER'S MARRIAGE

I was solely dedicated to help my mother through her grief. When I was a child growing up, there was a lady, Mrs. Redmond, who lived on the fifth floor walk up apartment. She drank heavily, and used to call me to go to the store to get her groceries. When she died, her husband, John Redmond, had her wake in Lynch's funeral parlor. Since he was a lonesome man, I walked down to the funeral parlor, with my dog, Cookie, tied to my baby carriage. My two children sat outside while I went to a chapel and since I didn't like looking at dead people, I closed my eyes and said a prayer, and I felt a tap on my shoulder, and John Redmond told me I was in the wrong chapel, and he escorted me to where she was interred.

I invited him to my home for dinner, and he fell in love with my mother. He used to take her out to dinner, and she was very happy. Shortly after they met, my mother announced that they were going to get married. Only my sister was invited to their wedding.

MOVING AGAIN

I started having problems with the landlord of the building. The people who rented to me moved and new owners took over the building. We decided to move again. Mama was no help to me with baby-sitting. She seemed to be doing all right with her new husband. I couldn't keep up with my job. Here I was, sick at heart in a bad marriage, trying to help my mother. Can you get the picture?

Barbara and Ricky and I were never made to feel welcome in my mother's house, or at my sister's. The dinners and parties were always at my house! Moving seemed like a good idea. Where to move presented a problem. We, rather I, decided on Rockaway Beach again. As I said, he was weak minded and went along when decisions were made for him. We rented a room and my two children and my husband stayed there. I found an apartment for a reasonable rental but we needed a refrigerator. As usual, it was up to me to get one. My passive aggressive husband disappeared and left me with two children.

A lady let her 14-year-old daughter baby-sit for me, so I could get a job. I got a job in Playland as a waitress. It was a real shabby place. You started working with a "bank" of your own money. When the place got really busy, the bartenders claimed you had not paid them. At the end of the night I had no money after making good tips.

I met Irene there. She had run away from home. She moved in with me and agreed to pay half of the rent. Irene had a daughter Barbie Ann. Barbie Ann, my son Ricky and my daughter, Barbara, seemed to get along well. Barbara was a very tiny baby and the rash she had was so severe, she used to cry a lot. I never suspected she had been molested. But good old Uncle Harry, with rosary in one hand, and his penis in the other, was molesting me as a child. I was very innocent in those days and really trusted everyone.

Irene's husband came to visit her and wanted her to come home with him. They had a beautiful home and they lived with her parents. The argument started because Irene used to steal the family liquor and get drunk. They wanted her back even under those conditions.

My family didn't know or care how I was or where I was. My two children were the first grand children in our family. My mother was busy with her husband, John, and my sister with her husband, Otto.

Somehow or another, Dick came home and he and Tony and Irene became friends. They invited Dick to go and live with them. He took my two children to their house and I became homeless once again.

JERRY THE ELECTRICIAN

I was working in the bar restaurant when I met Jerry, an electrician for the Playland Amusement Park. He felt sorry for me and took me out for some dinners. One night when he took me out, Dick reappeared on the scene.

He opened the door to Jerry's car and saw me kissing him and left. No fight no emotion that was visible in Dick! This was the beginning of my decent into a Hell of drinking to forget. I really had nothing to live for now. Up until this time I lived for my children. Now that Dick had taken them to live with Irene and Tony, I did not want to live anymore. I was homeless and Uncle Harry took me in and gave me a room in his apartment. Since I was not working, there was no food for me.

My cousin Arthur and Mary Ann lived up stairs and would call Uncle Harry up to her house for dinner. It was as if I didn't exist. Thus my title, "A Room Without Roaches, PLEASE!" dedicated to people like me with no self-esteem.

One night Uncle Harry came into my room and got into bed with me. He didn't have a chance to do anything because my cousin Arthur, came to the bedroom door and saw his father. Again I blamed myself for this incident. Jerry, the electrician, became my friend. He wanted to marry me and he introduced me to his mother. His mother was very hostile towards me. It was obvious she did not want her son involved with me. She was taking care of his children and I guess she was afraid I would replace her.

I just wanted my children back, but I was homeless and couldn't provide for them. My family was not willing to help my children or me. I knew that I had to go to work.

Uneducated and with no skills, where do you go? Back to the White Castle again. They always took me back because I was a good worker and they were a charitable organization. All the people I worked with were broken people. Women were divorced, alcoholics, and uneducated people.

We used to drink vodka and orange juice in a tiny out house to escape the rain and snow. I tried to rent an apartment from one of my co-workers, it didn't work out.

I desperately wanted my children back, and felt like I would marry anyone who would take my children and me. Jerry and I almost made it! I was always very Catholic in my beliefs. And the church got in our way, with the preaching, "Once a marriage is consummated, you cannot get a divorce." What a cruel joke, considering the way the priests were way back then, doing evil things, and not doing what they preached.

I was abused in my Catholic marriage. In those days, if you did get divorced, you could not be buried in consecrated ground. So I buried myself alive, and went and asked Dick to take me back.

I used to be allowed to see my children once a week. Since I had no car I used to stay outside a bar, Gilday and Healy's and look for men who had a car, so they would drive me over to see my children. My tips from the White Castle were used to buy them toys. One day my "so called" friend, Irene, told me I should buy their daughter, Bobby Ann gifts also. I replied, "I think your daughter has you and Tony and a new house. My children have nothing." Silent Dick never said a word.

After I picked up my children, we went to where I worked for hamburgers. As I said, my family never invited us for dinner. Their doors and their hearts were closed to their grand children and me. After each visit, I walked away and got very drunk to kill the pain. I learned that Uncle Harry wanted me at his house for his amusement; I really had nowhere else to go.

When I went to visit my mother, she would fix me a steak and say, "Hurry up and eat so John doesn't find out that I fed you." Nice to feel that you are not wanted.

I went to O'Connell's Bar where I used to work and John pulled me off the bar stool and knocked my teeth out. He was a powerful brute of a man who was on parole for various crimes.

The alcohol did not work for me any more. It could not kill the pain and losses of my life.

I knew that the only way I would get my children back was to go back to Dick. Now it was up to me to find housing and money for all of us.

UNCLE HARRY'S HOUSE

Back to Uncle Harry's house again. This time with Dick, Barbara and Ricky. We were all packed into one room, two to a bed. I was so happy to have my children back I would have done anything to keep the family together.

My cousin Arthur's wife did her usual mean routine of calling Uncle Harry up for dinner, but not us. What a mean spirited person she was! Very pretty outside but with a mean heart. Uncle Harry wanted to get rid of all of us. He kept saying his daughter, Sister Mary Henry was coming and he wanted us out of there. I can't say that I blamed him! Especially now that I had a husband and he couldn't molest me.

Arthur was very prosperous as a cop and he took good care of his family, Mary Ann and her two children. They always had enough to eat while we were homeless.

I knew now that it was up to me to look for an apartment. Dick was not about to do anything. I always closed my eyes to his indifference and blamed myself for his unhappiness. I always felt that everything was my fault. My mother's alcoholism, my father's death, I got a steady injection of guilt from the Catholic Church as well.

44 JOHNSON AVE

One day I saw an ad in the paper for an apartment in Williamsburg Brooklyn. The rent was very cheap, and it sounded good. The apartment was on the fifth floor in a dingy building. The superintendent asked me for a hundred dollars under the table. When Dick saw the place, he agreed that we should take it. I was so happy to have a place to take my two children to live. I adored my children and would do anything to keep them.

Dick went to work in the shipyards in Brooklyn, and even though we only had two twin beds to sleep all four of us. I was happy.

In those days there was a furniture store on Montrose Ave. and the owners extended credit to anyone in the neighborhood who needed furniture. I was able to furnish the whole apartment and pay a little down and make weekly payments.

What surprised me was that although the building was old and dingy, the tenants very poor, they would furnish their apartment lavishly. The inside of my home looked like rich people lived there.

My children wanted to go downstairs to play so I could look out the window and see them. At the time the streets were safe. Later on the neighborhood became dangerous.

I bought a sewing machine and used to make little dresses and playsuits for my little girl, Barbara. One night my mother and Uncle Harry came to visit me and brought me what looked like a ham. They were both convulsing with laughter and we hungrily ate what we thought was ham. After we finished eating Uncle Harry confessed that he stole the tongue from my next-door neighbor, Tom, who left his door open and fell asleep drunk while the tongue was cooking. Mama and Uncle Harry could not stop laughing. Dick did not think it was funny at all. My Irish family could always find a reason to laugh. At funerals and weddings they would gather and tell lies and laugh. My husband was English and came from a very serious family. I never saw him laugh and I never saw him cry. Somehow or another I inherited a sense of humor. It helped me transform tragedies into comedies. I was laughing on the outside and crying on the inside.

My next-door neighbor, Delores, also lived on the fifth floor. She had a son Gary and a daughter Patsy. She was separated from her husband and she worked in a factory. She used to call her husband and practically beg him for twenty-five dollars every week. She had a friend that we called Uncle Mike who helped her out financially. Delores and Mike and my husband and I did a great deal of family things together. One day we all went to the beach and my son Ricky wandered away from us. We looked all over for him and then when we finally did find him, he said that we were lost and had moved. This became a life long problem for Ricky, blaming others for his problems.

We were all close friends and the children played together. These were good times and I was so happy to be a family again. I tried not to notice my husband's indifference to me. There was always a shortage of money, so I got a job as a waitress in an Italian restaurant in Greenpoint. I was a very poor waitress and kept making mistakes. The boss told me he could only keep one waitress so I agreed to leave and let the other girl keep the job.

When I got home that night, I knocked and knocked on my door and smelled smoke. The air was filled with heavy black smoke. I went to my friend Delores and she let me in. Dick had fallen asleep with his cigarette and nearly killed my children and him. We all recovered and again it was up to me to solve the money problems we were having.

Many times when the peddler who sold me the furniture came to collect I did not have the money to pay him. The rent was cheap enough but we were always broke.

The building was a lively place. Most everyone kept their doors open. A lady used to baby-sit everyone's children while they were at work. She made a nice tax free living with about ten children. There was a good spirit in the building.

Another lady who was a friend of mine, used to give us all Italian bread, since her husband worked in a family bakery. I used to walk to Siegal Street Market and buy three pounds of chop meat for a dollar. I learned to make stuffed peppers, meatloaf and many other economical meals with the chopped meat and the free bread.

Every day my two children and I walked to the market, and people said friendly greetings to each other. My children were my whole life, and I used to take them for lunch when I could find the money to treat them.

Barbara Jean was a very smart little girl. I used to carry her down the five flights of stairs. We used to stop at Tillie and Sam Specter's apartment, as I said, the doors were open, and Barbara used to recite the names of the Spector family. She also counted all the beds and said that Tillie had ten beds. Tillie and her husband, Sam, owned the grocery store below their apartment. They used to give everyone credit. Whenever Mama and her new husband came I used to run up a big bill to entertain them. I loved my family and I was very good to my husband's family as well.

Not too many people wanted to visit us on the top floor, and since money was short, it was up to me to find a way to survive. The superintendent of my building told me there was a job in the next building. The salary was sixty dollars a month and free rent. I jumped at the chance to apply. Mr. Schiff hired my husband and me. I had no idea what I was getting into. I just needed a solution to our money problems, since Dick was always out of work.

At that time he worked at Red Hook shipyard, not far from my house. To this day I don't know why we never had enough money for food.

My cousin Arthur, the cop, said recently that Dick was a loser and never made a living. I guess I was blinded and so happy with my two children that I really never noticed how indifferent he was to me.

I would have settled for any kind of abuse just to have my children and some form of family life.

I never told anyone of my loneliness or sorrow. I went to daily Mass and Communion in Most Holy Trinity Church. I made friends with the nun there. She was also principle of the school, but I never confided in her about my life.

SUPERINTENDENT BUILDING 44

Here we are now in charge of a low-income twenty-five family building, heated with coal. Our job, which became my job, was to clean five flights of stairs weekly. With double landings, it was like ten flights. In order to heat the building I had to shovel the coal from the bin into the hot furnace, and stroke the furnace, to keep the building warm. I had to remove the clinkers from the hot furnace and shovel it into garbage cans and put the cans outside the building for the garbage men to pick up. That completed, I had to clean two alleyways, where the tenants, too lazy to bring the garbage down, threw it out the windows. This feat took all my strength. I only had one kidney.

Now Mr. Schiff, the landlord, came twice a month to collect his rents. Sometimes people would bring the rent down to my first floor apartment, but most of the time, I had to walk up the five flights of stairs to get it.

My one joy was that I had my two children, and could sit with them outside with the other mothers and watch them play. I was very happy with my family, although my silent husband seldom spoke to me. Sam Specter's grocery store provided for us, we could charge, and pay once a week.

Ricky was enrolled in Most Holy Trinity School, and Barbara and I walked him to school and I went to Mass. Sometimes I was covered with coal from the furnace, but I never missed Mass.

There were some characters living in the building. One husband and wife, who had two children, were afraid of the cold weather. They looked like ghosts and would not walk their dogs outside if it were winter. The dog did his duty outside my door and it used to stink inside my apartment. They said it was not their dog.

Another character, who was an alcoholic, had several children. Her husband came and went and left her with another child. She hung out at the corner bar and sometimes the kids were starving. Welfare gave her big blocks of cheese and bags of flour, which she promptly sold and drank up. Her last child was sleeping in a bedroom drawer. What a sad sight! The grocer's son and I had a raffle and bought her a crib. One little girl, Kathy, had lice in her hair and was often outside in the cold with very little clothing. A nun used to pass by and try to sew her dress and comb her hair.

I met a woman who had a son that she was sending to Phyllis Anderson School of Ballet and Tap Dancing, so I enrolled Barbara Jean. Ironically, it was very close to the St. George Hotel where my favorite uncle had jumped from the 25th floor to his death.

Barbara did well and went weekly to rehearse for a school play. I was so excited and proud. I invited Dick's family, Bea and Jim, and my mother and stepfather to see my little girl dancing on the stage. I can see her now in her Hawaiian outfit, singing and dancing to the tune of "Lovely Hula Hands". My family kept complaining that it took too long to see her in the final act.

These were the best days of my broken life. My pride and joy was in my children. Later on in life, I was to see these children sticking needles in their arms, become heroin addicts and go to jail.

As time went by the neighborhood began to deteriorate. There were gang wars between the Puerto Ricans and their rival gangs. The streets were not safe. Tempers would flair up at night and they would pull off the garbage can lids, fight and run. I spoke to my friend, Sister Catherine Joseph, and told her I was planning on moving. She said that we were giving up the fight and leaving the neighborhood to the warriors. I feared for my children's lives, not the community.

The work was really exhausting and I was pregnant with my third child, Robert. My husband was always out of work and we never had enough money. I took in children to mind while their parents were at work. This provided food money. I always had to take the lead. So I asked the landlord to give my husband a job painting apartments. He agreed to pay Dick $25.00 a room. We bought paint for $1.00 a gallon and we were in the painting business.

The tenants had been waiting for three years to get their apartment painted. In those days the popular colors were deep rose coral and forest green. Dick had to buy color paste and mix with cheap white paint. This added to the cost of the paint. He was a messy, spiteful man and came home laughing and told me he had painted cockroaches rose and green. He hated all the people in the building and they would call me and say: "He painted my pictures on the wall. This is a painter?"

Time went on and I put away every penny I could in order to get out of Williamsburg. I finally accumulated a few thousand dollars and went house hunting. By this time I was very pregnant with my son, Robert, and I still had to shovel coal and clean the halls. One time my stepfather, John, helped me and carried my mop bucket up five flights of stairs.

Another time my uncle, Harry, came and saw me shoveling the coal in the cellar. He said: "I would rather see you as a prostitute in the street than doing this work." So much for his sentiment. You see he treated his wife like a queen so he could not understand Dick allowing me to do this job.

We went house hunting on Long Island every Sunday. Driving my children to look at pretty houses and flowers on Long Island were happy times. When I returned to the dirty street and gang wars I became very determined to give my children a better life.

My mother and stepfather said they would like to move in with us. You must remember that at one time, no one would take my children or me in. I loved my mother and stepfather, so I agreed.

At this time I found out that I was pregnant again. Since I was very Catholic and they allowed no birth control, I knew that I could not bring my child into this neighborhood. I was also afraid of having a miscarriage since I had no help with the coal shoveling or the cleaning of the halls. My husband as usual showed no emotions when I told him I was expecting a child, despite the evidence to the contrary I wanted this marriage to work. Daily Mass and Communion helped me to stay in this dysfunctional life style. I never told anyone how unhappy I was. My friend Sister Catherine Joseph was not a person you could confide in.

45 MAGAW PLACE

One Sunday afternoon Dick and I went to a real estate agent. He began showing us houses. Because my mother and stepfather wanted to live with us, I began looking for a four-bedroom house.

The house I decided on had two bedrooms downstairs and two bedrooms upstairs. Thinking my mother and stepfather would live upstairs, this was our choice.

My family was to give me half of the down payment when it came time to move, but then they decided they did not want to live with us after all.

What a financial mess they created. We barely had enough money to rent a trailer and make the required down payment. At the closing of the deal, Dick and I walked away with just enough to buy some hamburgers.

I was so happy to have a real home with roses and flowers for my children, that we went outside and lay on the grass while the children carved their initials on a tree. The sellers had not done a lot of work themselves so it needed a lot of remodeling and redecorating.

I took Ricky to the school that he was to attend. He said: "I am not moving", so I applied some psychology to the issue and said, "OK, you can stay at Johnson Avenue and we will move here". He changed his mind very quickly. I was still very Catholic and I tried to get them into St. Joseph's Catholic School where I felt the quality of education would be better. However, they were not admitted and little Barbara was too young for first grade.

I started remodeling and decorating my house. I tore walls down. In those days no one locked their doors. Neighbors used to stop and remark how beautiful the house looked. I planted beautiful daffodils and tulips. They used to take flowers to put on the altar. Daily Mass and Communion sustained me and despite the fact that my husband was never around, my family was doing well. We said a rosary each night at eight.

I became very active in the church. I joined the Legion of Mary and the Apostles of Good Will. My home became a center for teaching little children and preparing them for their first Communion. My husband did not like this idea so eventually I gave up the teaching.

I tried desperately to get Dick to go to church and take some part in the Catholic Church. He remained apart and was isolated from the children and me.

One priest asked me to be the chairman for the Apostles of Good Will. I took this over very happily. My job was to visit the sick, dying and fallen away Catholics. Little did I know that soon I would be "fallen away".

One family I visited was Italian. It was a second marriage. The man, Arnie, and his wife were married outside the Catholic Church. Annie and I made many weekly visits to encourage them to come back to church. When Arnie was dying, we called Father Richardson to his bedside.

As Arnie was carried into the church, his wife thanked me and said this is Arnie's first time in a church, thanks to you. I hope Arnie will speak a good word for me in heaven.

Another woman, Marie and her daughter, were not going to church. When Annie and I visited Marie, she had a leak in her plumbing. I jokingly said, "Marie, you don't need us, you need a plumber". Marie and I became friends. She had lupus, and was involved in a dysfunctional relationship with her cousin. She went to church and died in peace.

There were many families that I was involved with that returned to God. In the meantime, my family was getting further away from God.

The church had a habit of calling me to assist with the sick and the dying. I'm not that sure what the priests were doing with their spare time, but my phone rang off the hook with parish calls for help.

One couple I became very attached to was the Kelly family. They were an elderly Irish family that needed some support and also assistance with daily living. Mr. and Mrs. Kelly were the parents of a son and daughter, who would have nothing to do with them. My son,

Robert, was a little boy and I used to walk with him several blocks to the Kelly's to cook their favorite meal and sing Irish songs to them. Anna B. and another woman became involved with the family, and tried to help them.

Around this time, the pastor, who had a severe drinking problem, gave a dinner for all the volunteers in the parish. My friend, Anne had a deep friendship with one of the priests, so he made her head of the Apostles of Good Will, and I became the chairman of the sick and the dying. Anne was a social butterfly, who liked to drink and party. She would have done well with Our Lady of Grace Society, a social club, but did not belong in a serious situation.

She liked to party and to go on vacations, so she decided to withdraw from the Kelly family, and make their children take responsibility. The children did not want to be bothered with their parents.

Shortly after that, Mrs. Kelly died. Robert, my son, and I went to visit, but Mr. Kelly was getting senile and did not realize his wife was dead. He used to tell me not to sing or make noise, as I would wake up his wife.

The children finally gave a funeral for their mother, and the daughter spoke bitterly about her mother.

The day of the funeral Mass, they walked to the back of the church to exit and Mr. Kelly broke away from the children, and came over to kiss me and thank me.

What a bonus that was for me. Meanwhile our chairman did not attend the funeral; she was off vacationing in New Jersey.

The priest came to her house nightly and they drank together, while her husband worked two jobs.

Finally the Apostles of Good Will disbanded and they were no more. In the meantime, my family was falling apart while I ran out to help other people. I did not know how to say "NO" to any request for help.

My son, Robert, was a baby and I used to take him to Mass every morning. He was a very well behaved child, and he was very attached to me. I can see him now in a white snowsuit, holding his favorite stuffed animal, a bunny.

There was very little fathering at this time so he used to beg me to pick him up. People said they thought he was attached to my hip. I adored my three children and tried to be a mother and a father to them.

The usual jealousy between siblings was present. My Ricky and Barbara were convinced that I loved Robert more than them. In order to get even, they used to put salt on Robert's ice cream. All this was done in family fun. We really had a good time together. Someday I hope they will remember this.

One day they put Robert in a trunk and they took him out and made him scream, while they threw the empty trunk down the stairs. I nearly had a heart attack thinking my baby, Robert, was in the trunk.

My husband never took part in any of the family activities. Barbara and Ricky were both in Scouts. I was exhausted showing up for the club meetings. I tried to be their mother and their father.

I knew my children needed a role model, so I enrolled Ricky in Altar Boys. The man training these boys was a dedicated father and a family man. He trained Ricky in the Latin Mass. By the time Ricky learned Latin, the mass was in English.

My life and my whole existence was for my children's betterment and the community, but mainly the Catholic Church. If I had only known how this Church, through one of their priests, would come into my home and demoralize my family.

My friends were also church volunteers. My best friend was Anne. We were like sisters. As I wrote earlier, she became the head of the Apostles of Good Will, but did not like the role.

Anne was always in my home, and my children loved her. Her husband was a policeman and worked as a roofer to keep Anne in a nice lifestyle. She had two children and justified this by saying, "the holy family had only one child".

My son, Robert, and I went to daily Mass and Communion. He also accompanied me on my home visits to the sick and dying. He had a favorite stuffed animal that was missing one eye. He called him Binny. One day, while riding in the car, he held Binny out the window and Binny got lost. I tried to backup on the Southern State Parkway to get Binny, but to no avail.

Later on in life, when my son was stationed in Korea, I sent him a Teddy Bear in memory of Binny. At this time he is Master Sergeant Robert Howells.

My mother and step-father, John, used to visit us weekly. Dick was working on the Long Island Railroad and my mother and John could ride free. This was a problem with mother's kidney function at this time. She never made it to the bathroom on the train.

They liked to come to my home for a fabulous dinner and they had their own room in the home they were to live in. I truly loved my stepfather and got along very well with him.

Since my husband was never around, John and I used to take a bus to the local A&P Store. While I shopped for food John went to the bar next door and told me not to tell my mother. I knocked on the bar window when I was ready to go home. This was our little secret.

Meanwhile my mother was pouring water in the liquor bottle so no one would know she drank the liquor.

These were happy times because I loved my family and tried to create a loving atmosphere.

John felt sorry for me because he saw the danger in my house. Wires were running across the floor and he could not understand that Dick did not seem to care about anything. In my mother's small apartment John was very careful and kept fixing things.

Robert was getting older and I, being very Catholic, became pregnant again. Rhythm was the keynote in those days.

My church friend gave me a big shower at Blanch and Mike's house. They were close friends of mine. Mike used to take me shopping with him because Dick was never around. My mother and John could not believe the wonderful gifts I got for my unborn child.

As we opened each gift my mother said "I'll give you $100 but you must give it back to me and John". My mother had just come back from a trip to Ireland and always had money so it was not a case of her being poor, just poor in spirit.

ROBERT'S BIRTH

My beloved son Robert was born after Christmas on January 14th. He was a handsome little guy and has a son today who looks just like him.

Mama decided to visit and help me. She was no help at all and burned things in the house. She had very little control of her kidneys and used to wet all over the house.

I had to beg her to get up and just give the new baby one bottle during the night. My husband once again was unavailable. I was over whelmed trying to be a mother and a father to three children.

Robert gave me much joy and he was a very good baby. Dick never paid attention to my children or me.

MY STEPFATHER'S DEATH

Shortly after John's baby shower, my stepfather felt sick. They were driven home by my husband, and John entered St. John's Hospital with a cold. It was Halloween, "Trick or Treat". He died in the elevator. My mother was beside herself with grief. She had lost two good men now.

I was about due to have my fourth child. My sister took Mama to her house to make funeral arrangements. I tried to phone to find out where he was waked, but again my sister would not tell me.

My neighbor, Mike, offered me a ride to the funeral parlor to see if he was waked at Ed. Lynch's in Sunnyside. My sister-in-law, Bea, offered to meet me because Dick was not available. Bea and I went to my sister's house but she would not let us in to see my mother. We stood outside and I cried. I always internalized the pain and thought it was my fault.

Bea and I went to the funeral parlor and my mother never came. Uncle Harry asked me where she was. I made excuses to all the people that Mama was sick. Mama was so doped up she never made the first night of the funeral. The next night my mother showed up crying and all doped up with pills.

I felt a deep sorrow at John's death. He was a good man, and my children loved him. My husband never reached out to me or said a word of comfort. I'm not sure how he felt about John's death if anything at all. He seemed to distance himself from all human feelings. No one could get into his life, or figure him out.

We all met at St. Theresa's Church where the funeral Mass was said for John. When the Mass was over, my mother, my sister, and her two children got into the funeral car and there was no room for my family or me.

After the funeral, we rode to the cemetery. My sister and my mother, and again there was no room for me. By this time I was eight months pregnant with my son, John, and feeling very sick. My husband took Barbara's hand and I waddled along side of them, totally lost in my grief.

The burial was over now, and I was soon to give birth to my son, John. Christmas was approaching and I needed to do shopping for my three children. Blanche came with me. She was my neighbor and a friend. I had a charge in Gimball's, so away we went, with me barely fitting under the wheel of my car, I was so big.

Dick was somewhere in Brooklyn, I'm not sure where. I was so happy with my home and my children and having a room of my own, that I really did not miss him.

My children were in Boy Scouts, Girl Scouts and Altar Boys and I was actively visiting sick families, so my time was spent in community work. I knew there was something missing, and that my friend's lives were different than mine. I didn't have to look too far to see that just across the street were Blanche and Mike. Mike used to take Blanche and me grocery shopping every Thursday. As I look back now, they were very kind to my family and me.

We spent many Sundays together eating and drinking. I was always welcome in their house. This was a sharp contrast to my mother. Blanche's mother lived in Harlem, and we spent New Year's Eve with her. Blanche used to come home from her mother's house laden with gifts. My mother never gave us Christmas gifts or recognized my birthday. I was very jealous of Blanche. She seemed to have everything I didn't have.

JOHN'S BIRTH

My son was to be named John at Mama's request. I took my neighbor, Blanche, Christmas shopping in Gimbel's because I had a charge account there. As we ascended the escalator, a woman's foot got stuck and when I helped her, my water seemed to break. I called the doctor and he said to come to the hospital.

I was in the labor room when I could feel John's head coming out. Doctor M. quickly crossed my legs, because he wanted me in the Delivery Room. Years later I learned that this blocked the air off to John, causing anoxia. However I knew very little about medical problems since I dropped out of school at sixteen years of age.

John was a hyperactive baby, weighing in at five pounds. When my church friends came to see him, they teased me, and said he was so blonde, he looked like Mr. Kelly, the elderly man I visited for nine months. We all had a good laugh about that.

I used to get up from my hospital bed to gaze at John every few hours. He was a beautiful baby and I adored him. One night the guard on duty saw me admiring my baby and he asked if this was my first child. When I told him it was my fourth, he was astonished. Not too many mothers displayed such love for their fourth child.

Ricky and Dick came to take John home and me. Ricky dressed John. When we got home, I dressed John in his Santa Claus suit and laid him in Barbara's arms. He became Barbara's doll baby until tragedy entered my home!

It seemed that I let the wrong people into my home and my heart. Coincidentally, the parish was located at 666 Allen Ave. The three sixes. I'm not sure if this had any significance in my life, or my children's lives. We appeared to be a happy family to the external world. This was not the truth. Since I was so heavily involved in church work, it was important to project a happy image.

My life was centered around the Catholic Church and my phone rang incessantly, because the parish priests were not available. The had an answering service long before any one knew about answering services. The burden of the sick calls and the dying came to my home.

Our Pastor had a serious drinking problem. He was a brilliant writer and a highly educated man, but the alcohol had beaten him down. He was taken to Good Samaritan Hospital and when my friend Anne and I visited him he was very upset that one of the Priests had called the Bishop, and his family doctor had diagnosed him as a chronic alcoholic. He was happy to see Anne, and me and we made some jokes about lighter matters.

When he went back home to the rectory, people were aware of his problem, and this did not help him at all. Meanwhile my family was struggling with the absence of a father and a mother who was constantly missing; doing church work, and making home visits to a sick and dying population. I did not realize my family was sick also.

My friends really made a big fuss over Johnny. He was handsome with blonde curls, and very smart. He adored Barbara and she took over the mother role in the family.

ENTER THE JESUITS

The pastor hired two Jesuit priests, Father L and Father N, both from Spain. Father L could not speak English so another priest had to decipher his homilies. He was attending New York University and the Jesuit Order was paying for his education. He did not drive and had no car, so I usually drove him since I attended daily Mass with my son, Robert.

Every one was in awe of this priest and his incoherent message. He was studying political science at this time and was a brilliant scoundrel. He was good at manipulating the parishioners who were thrilled to have him for dinner. He had many invitations. One home in particular hosted many parties for him. There was guitar playing and lots of food and alcohol. Father L did not drink much, but Father N did and had to be taken back to the rectory and called at 6:30 to say his Mass.

We all thought that was strange. We did not know about alcoholism.

My husband was gone most of the time so these "so called" friends filled a lonesome void in my life. They came to my house and partied all the time. I had an open invitation, open house and especially an open heart.

After John's birth we purchased a player piano. I was trying to imitate the B family and also give my children piano lessons.

I planned a great christening for my newborn son, John. All the guests had a great time. They drank and partied all night. The two priests that came drank very heavily. The next morning they were still there. Meanwhile, back at 666 Parish, significant to the devil, the two Spanish Jesuit Priests were going to New York University and also saying Mass at the Church.

The pastor declared one house off limits to these priests.

At this time Father L could speak a little English. Everyone was thrilled to provide him a ride to Mass and invite him to dinner, including me.

He was a student of political science and clever and manipulative. May God have mercy on him for ruining my family and abusing my children and me.

He gained entrance to my home on the pretense of giving my son, Ricky, tutoring for his courses at Saint John the Baptist School.

Every Sunday we dined him and left him in the bedroom with Ricky. I stupidly thought he was a good role model or at least better than his father who provided money, but nothing else.

Dick disappeared for months at a time. He claimed he was working on ships as a boilermaker.

I was engrossed in church work and helped many families, but neglected my own.

Father L came to my home every Sunday. I considered him a role model and never guessed what his game plan was.

"BEWARE OF DEVILS WHO ROAM THE EARTH SEEKING TO RUIN SOULS".

Because of my early marriage, I had little education and was not experienced in child raising nor the evil ways of the world. Father L shared with me some things about his life, such as an aunt who was sexual with him. He told me that certain smells would "turn him on" when he was hearing confessions. I was in awe of him and valued his friendship. I appreciated the fact that he was tutoring my son, but now I wonder what my son learned behind that closed bedroom door.

By this time the Pastor was a seriously sick alcoholic. Someone wrote to the Bishop about his drinking. He was taken out of the rectory in an ambulance bleeding from every pore in his body.

When my friend, Anne, and I visited him in the hospital, he was very angry with the doctor who wrote a diagnosis of acute chronic alcoholism. Only Anne and I were permitted to visit him. He did not trust anyone and was very bitter about being hospitalized.

Meanwhile the two Jesuits were living in the rectory and going to school in New York. Father L was living in the rectory, dining with the parishioners and collecting a salary. He also got a cut on the Masses that were said for the dead. He told me one family was so happy to have him for dinner they served lobster and they drank very heavily. After dinner he came to my house to study his homily for Mass—or so he said.

My neighbor began to wonder why Father L was at my house so often although my husband was away most of the time.

Most of the time I had no idea where my husband was. He left me a small amount of money in a bedroom dresser drawer and I never questioned him as to what he made. I have never felt that I deserved any of the good things in life so all my life I have put up with all kinds of abuse.

A family gave Father L a small car, as he had no transportation. Little did they know that this was to be his "getaway" car. He transferred to St. Rose Di Lima Parish but still attended New York University.

Father L talked me into giving him a "going away" party before he left our Lady of Grace. The party took place in Blanche D's house across the street from my house.

It was a gala affair and well attended by most of the parishioners. All gave him money to help with his school expenses.

My husband, Dick, claimed he was working on ships and was nowhere in sight. Father L knew this but kept coming to my home to tutor my son, Ricky, and have dinner with the family. I trusted him and wanted him as a good role model for Ricky.

One day Father L asked me to drive him upstate to apply for a teaching job.

I had an old Ford car with a lot of mileage on it, but I drove him many miles to Oneonta College. He had his "going away" money with him and he was very secretive about the amount he had received.

At this time my husband came and went. We were approaching Christmas and he had been gone for months.

As I wrote previously, Father L transferred to Saint Rose Di Lima parish but was very unhappy there. He was convinced that the pastor was stealing his rightful share of the Mass money. Each priest received a stipend for the Mass they offered up for the dead.

Father L had a charismatic personality. Everyone was in awe of him and his pseudo sancity. A parishioner gave him a Toyota as a gift. Little did they know this was to be his "get-a-way" gift.

He manipulated everyone he met. He sat my four children down and told them he wanted to help the family since their father was not around.

Father L came to my house weekly while my husband was somewhere in Brooklyn or on a ship. Father L left St. Rose Di Lima and went to live in New York City to be close to New York University.

THE AUTOMOBILE ACCIDENT

My best friend Anne's father suffered from acute alcoholism. He had been carried out of his apartment and taken to a hospital in Ozone Park. Anne came to my house crying. Since she had a title in Our Lady of Grace she did not want anyone to know of her father's condition.

I left my four children in my daughter Barbara's care and took Anne to the hospital. This involved putting tires on my Rambler car and driving her nightly to watch her father die. She seemed to take it more lightly than I did. I watched her eat a ham sandwich while the crumbs fell on her father's deathbed.

Anne was very close to my family and me. She was always at my home. I welcomed her and we did many house calls together. Her husband, Jim, was a devoted father and a loving husband working as a police officer and also as a roofer. She was very comfortable financially and had accumulated a large amount of telephone stock.

On the last night of her father's wake she was making jokes about how she put a six-pack of beer and a newspaper in his casket. Everyone was very amused by her jokes.

After the wake I was to drive home with two friends. My friend, his wife and I had been drinking. The driver of the "death car" was drunk and crashed into another car on the turnpike in Flushing Lights and police cars were at the scene.

I am not sure if I were thrown out of the car or how I got onto the road. I crawled across the street to an apartment with lights on. A man admitted me and let me phone home to my children who were along.

The other passenger, Anne Agate, was in the back seat also. The police took me to the nearest hospital where they X-rayed my head. I would not stay in the hospital and wait until the X-rays dried. They saw that my skull was fractured, but I refused to let them admit me until I got home to my children. I felt that they were fatherless and if I stayed in the hospital, they would be motherless too.

G and M drove me home covered with blood and a black eye on my left side. My children saw me leave our house all dressed up and then I was carried back into the house half dead. I was laid in my daughter's down stairs bedroom and left to die. My children were terrified at the sight of me.

The next day my friend's father was buried. After the burial my "so called friends" came to my house. Dr. Shaw, the family doctor, was called. When he looked at the X-rays he determined that the left side of my skull was severely fractured and he wanted me in the hospital. I had no insurance and my children would have been on their own. My husband was not around as usual. The church friends came and brought me meals and tried to keep me awake. My best friend Anne discouraged my other friends from coming. They took over my house. I had made many friends in the church because I was so active and got to know many good people. Anne, being the boss, would not allow visitors other than herself and M.

Many years later I learned that the left side of the brain, which was where mine was injured, controls logic. My head was dented and they found fragments of bone pressing on the blood vessels leading to the brain. I was totally out of it with loss of hearing and a black eye. What a sight for my poor children. Up until that time I was their hero Mom who made fabulous dinners and provided wonderful Christmas presents. Now it was close to Christmas and there was no money for food or gifts and my husband was missing.

The Jesuit Priest, Father L, came to the house to give me the last rites. I remember waking up in my daughter's bedroom with him staring at me, and then blacking out again. My skull was severely fractured and my heart was broken.

I kept going in and out of blackouts and the Priest kept putting a spoon to my mouth. I do not know what else he may have done to me, but I know that because he was a priest, I trusted him and felt that he could do no wrong. At this time he was living in the Leo House in New York City and calling me every night. He would come to my house and stay late into the morning. He would always stay longer than any other friends. People were wondering what this was all about.

About this time the Pastor declared Mrs. B.'s house off limits and forbade the priests to go there. There were serious problems with another priest in the rectory who later became a cab driver. He and the Pastor had serious drinking problems. But we did not mention that. We swept it under the rug and pretended nothing was wrong.

I had no insurance of any kind. Dr. Elber told me my skull was severely fractured and splinters of bone were pressing on the blood vessel leading to the brain.

One day an insurance man came to my house while I was in and out of blackouts. I felt like my head was split in two parts. I could not hear or understand what he said but I vaguely remember signing some papers. Until this day I do not know what I signed.

Anne B. brought her friends to my house while I lay on the couch. They had good times playing my player piano. They ate and drank and then left my children and me. I put on a good show. I was good at pretending.

Johnny was a baby and no one offered to help me with him. Barbara took over the house and became the mother of the family.

People from the church came in the front and back doors and partied until all hours of the night. I was so happy to have friends that I tried to forget about my head injury. I was afraid if I improved they would leave and I would have no one.

THE FATHER RETURNS

Dick came home Christmas Eve with a story that he had no money for Christmas. He wanted to use my charge card at A&S and buy presents. I refused. He had been gone for months and did not bring a thing home with him for the children or me. No money because he had been arrested in Texas and also had another family in Brooklyn. I was too afraid to ask him any questions, thus "MY ROOM WITHOUT ROACHES PLEASE".

I told him that I had been in an accident, which was very obvious since my head on the left side was dented in and still is. My eyes were all black and blue. Again, he had no reaction. I told him that the doctor told me to start a lawsuit since I was severely hurt. I also told him that he was entitled to what they called "loss of services" as my husband. He showed no interest in his children or me. I told him I would no longer tolerate his indifference to his children and me.

My four children, including baby John, were sitting on the couch when he left and took a hotel room somewhere.

The next day was Christmas. Some friends came and brought Christmas presents. The priest, Father L, also came and brought some gifts. I was in great pain mentally and physically. My husband came later in the day and took my four children to my sister's house, a very sick, evil place to take children.

When they left I called the priest I trusted and he came and took me for a ride upstate where he would be teaching. I called my sister to see if my children and husband were safe. She said they were all there. I was not happy that he took them to my sister's house. My sister was very mean to my mother and used to push her into a chair until my mother wet her pants. She always took money from my mother and treated her with disrespect whenever my mother was drunk, which was most of the time after my stepfather's death.

My husband came back with my children and asked me to drive him to Brooklyn. My son, Ricky, and I drove him, me with my fractured skull and broken heart.

When I got back home I found a loan book in my pocket book. He had taken out a loan for $4,000 and co-signed my name.

I called my friend the priest, and he advised me to call my husband's sister, Bea, and tell her that I would have her brother arrested. She said "mail me the book and I will pay the loan". Before I had called my husband's sister, I had taken the book to the bank with my forged signature. The president acknowledged that it was not my signature and advised that I should go to court. My best friend, the priest, was advising me how to do certain things.

In the meantime my son, Ricky, was kicked out of St. John the Baptist School, partly because of his behavior, but also because I could not pay the $30.00 a month. I was heart broken. I had pulled all kinds of strings to get Ricky into St. John the Baptist. Father N, another so called friend, intervened and Ricky was reinstated, but he was in bad shape after his father left. His behavior, coupled with my lack of funds, caused his expulsion.

I trusted the priest with my life and my children and I took his advice in all areas of my life. I thought he was a friend. I am reminded of the prayer of St. Michael, "BEWARE OF THE DEVILS WHO ROAM THE EARTH SEEKING THE RUIN OF SOULS."

When I let some people into my home and my heart, they betrayed me. My "so called church friends" came and ate and drank and partied at my home. They played my player piano and when my husband and my money were gone—they were gone. When the music stopped and the party stopped and poverty stepped in, the fair weather friends left.

I was in physical bad shape due to the skull fracture, which was left unattended.

Dr. Shaw knew that I had no money and he also felt that surgery would be dangerous. The fragments of bone pressing on the blood vessels to the brain, complicated by my having only one kidney would make surgery a high-risk situation.

Dr. Shaw recommended his relative, a lawyer, whom felt he could get me the money I deserved for my injury. I went to the lawyer and explained my case. He said that he would sue for $100,000 since my baby, John, was one year old and I was severely injured and had loss of hearing on my left ear. It sounded hopeful to me.

UPSTATE KINGSTON NEW YORK

My "so called friend", Father L., kept visiting my home and told my children he would take care of us since their father left.

They sat on the couch in deep sorrow, but he gave them hope that we could survive. He explained that he had a teaching job and he would help us financially. There was a heavy price to be paid. Since I was out of touch with reality I moved out of my house. After seeing a real estate agent I rented my house getting one month's rent and a month's security deposit. I rented a bungalow in Palenville with the money and paid my long overdue one-month mortgage.

My four children and I stayed in this motel and were still visited once a week by the man we trusted, Father L. I got a part time job as a waitress in an Italian restaurant. Due to the skull fracture, my hearing was impaired and one day the owner fired me. I was unaware that I had been fired and went to work the next day to hear that he had hired someone else.

I applied for another job as a waitress at the Rock Face Diner. My son, Ricky, also worked there. Barbara, my daughter, took care of my other two sons. Johnny was a baby and Robert was also young. The hours I worked at the diner were from 11pm until 7 in the morning. I was so sick that I used to fall asleep at the counter. The pay was very little but it kept us in food and paid the rent on the shack we lived in.

I took in a woman, who had a small child, to live with me. This was a financial loss and real emotional stress. I had to ask her to leave. We were crowded in the bungalow. She went with her boy friend and I thanked God when she was gone.

The pain from the injury on the left side of my head was very severe.

The priest came to visit and brought us some groceries. Barbara filled the basket. She never liked nor trusted him.

I met another abandoned lady who had one child. She rented the poolside concession for the summer.

A kind neighbor man used to play with Johnny. The Priest had nothing but contempt for John. One night John painted our cat with white shoe polish, and the Priest severely reprimanded him.

Rita, who became my best friend, used to look after John while he walked on the edge of the pool. I was exhausted after working all night at the diner and she gave him nickels for games while I tried to sleep.

Father L. used to bring rum to the shack. One night he got Ricky drunk and gave him my car to drive. We ended up in a ditch and the "so called priest" thought this was funny.

The priest took Ricky to sleep at the nice house he had rented close to Oneonta school where he was teaching. His landlord had to beg him for his monthly rent. He was used to living in parish houses free and getting dinners and donations of cars from the parishioners who felt honored to have a priest in their home. Little did they know that they were entertaining the devil himself.

THE CAR ACCIDENT

One night a knock came at my door, Father L., was outside. His black robes were on my lawn chair, and he was severely hurt. He had been given a small Toyota by the OR. Family and he had had an automobile accident.

I drove him to the Catskill hospital and he was admitted. He begged me to see that the story was not in the newspapers because he was returning every Sunday to say Mass in Saint Rose De Lima, in Amityville and collecting money for the Masses he offered. He led a double life, one as a priest and another as a teacher. He never separated the collar from the dollar. May God have mercy on you Father L., wherever you are.

My family and I went to visit him nightly in the hospital. One day when we went to visit him, his newly found friends, fellow teachers, were gathered in the hall, and they asked who I was. He never introduced me, but said: "She's just a woman who drove me here." It was a sad feeling but it put our relationship into perspective. Thus the title of this story, "A Room Without Roaches, PLEASE!" It depicts a woman, me, who not only had low self-esteem, but also had NO self-esteem.

Life had so beaten me down, that I thought I deserved nothing. It was easy to find people who reinforced that belief.

Today, as I do a behavior modification program with homeless women, I tell them to be sure they don't write their life story with a different Parker pen. "Beware of the devils who roam the earth seeking the ruin of souls."

After Father L. was released from Catskill hospital, he asked me to drive him to where his car was in the ditch. When we got there, the steering wheel was so twisted, that it was a miracle that he ever survived the accident.

His only comment was that he lost one shoe, from Spain, and how much it would cost him to purchase a new car. I should have sensed that this man was not a godly person, nor what he pretended to be.

Within a short time he purchased another car, and did not need any more rides to the bank or to the doctor's. His visits diminished to the family. He also disappeared for Christmas, in order to avoid giving holiday gifts.

I had to take my oldest son, Ricky out of school to help support our family. He got a job locally and Barbara became the head of the household.

In the meantime Father L. got an apartment near Oneonta School; and was fully employed, but still collecting Mass stipends at Saint Rose Di Lima. He had the better of two worlds while my family was straying nearby.

ENG'S RESTAURANT

I began looking for a job in the nearest town. There was a Chinese restaurant that was hiring waitresses. I was hired to work all different hours and I was happy to get the job.

By now I sensed this man meant only evil for my family and me. He hated Johnny and used to punish him for minor things.

We lived on a mountain in Palenville and it snowed very heavily. I used to travel 25 miles in hazardous weather to get to work at Eng's restaurant. Sometimes I had to put tire chains on my car and then remove them before getting into town, as they were illegal.

Many times the state troopers pulled me over for having bald tires. My fear was that I would not live to get home to my four children in the deserted mountain top shack.

I wrote to my mother for help to get back home. Other members of my family ignored my pleas for help.

After traveling the many miles to my job at Eng's restaurant, I knew that I needed to find a place closer to the job.

One night the boss invited us all out for drinks at the local bar. My friend and coworker, Shirley, and I went across the street to the bar.

Suddenly a snowstorm started and the road to my desolate home on the mountain, was declared closed. What should I do? My children were alone. There was some food in the house, thanks to the Chinese cook, Lee, who always gave me leftovers from the restaurant.

I called the state trooper in the area and asked him to tell my children that I was stuck down town in Kingston. They told me my children were OK.

All of a sudden the priest came into the bar. He tried to persuade me to go home with him. My girl friend, Shirley, and I went into the bathroom and I cried for my children. I no longer cared about the priest and his collar. I told her that he was a priest. She grabbed my shoulder and looked deeply into my eyes and told me "He is not a priest, he is a devil". She was right.

I slept on Shirley's floor that night and went home to my four children the next day. My children were attending a local school in the area. It was a one-room school for all ages. No one was learning very much.

Since we lived up a mountain, my children got on a bus early in the morning to attend classes. Many days they did not attend.

After I finished work at Eng's restaurant, I could not get my car up the steep hill. I used to walk few steps and fall down. My only concern was to get my tips, which would buy food for the next day.

I met many women also abandoned by their husbands or lovers.

My co-worker, Barbara McG, told me about an apartment close to Eng's restaurant. After spending a lonely Christmas with my four children, I knew that this "so called" priest was not going to help me. My boss gave me a Christmas tree and I found a charge account that allowed me to buy Christmas presents for my children.

Father L disappeared. He came to visit after Christmas. He told me his good friend, Father Rodriguez, was coming to visit him for a while. I met them both in a bar near his house. Father Rodriguez told me about a nun who was in love with him. They both left to go to Father L's house. I guess they bragged about their conquest.

Father L came to visit with empty hands and ate often at our house. He hated my baby, John, and was devoid of love for anyone he never contributed financially to our family, hated his landlord because he had to pay for rent. What a spoiled priest. The pastor of St. Rose Di Lima still gave him stipends for the Masses he offered and he was convinced the pastor was cheating on him.

One night my father appeared to me in a dream. He was shaking his head in disapproval of the life that I was leading. I knew my father, who rarely spoke to me in his entire life, was now at last communicating to me from the grave.

Another day while I was laying on the beach in Kingston, a lady whom I had waited on, woke me up to tell me about her broken heart. There were any people on the beach. Why me?

She told me her daughter was going with a priest. She and her husband were heart broken. I never told her my story, but I felt that God had sent her to me to wake from my nightmare.

MY APARTMENT ON HANRATTY STREET

A waitress told me that she was vacating her apartment close to my job. I also felt like it was closer to home. No one in my family seemed to call or send me any financial help to get home.

The apartment was in a dingy dark neighborhood. I saw some homeless men nearby. It was a poverty stricken neighborhood. However, I was on the first floor and my children would have a yard to play in.

The people, who lived upstairs, soon made me aware that they did not want children in their yard. They always complained about the noise we made. My children were very well behaved, so it was just a way to harass me. My friend, who had told me about the apartment, told me that they made her life miserable also, and that was why she moved.

Meanwhile, I made other friends, Louise and Al. My son Johnny used to play with their child.

Due to my long work hours at Eng's restaurant, I over slept one morning and John decided to drive my car. It was parked on a hill and he drove down the hill while a neighbor screamed and screamed seeing a little midget behind the wheel. We retrieved the car at the foot of the hill and neither John nor the car was hurt.

John used to dress himself in Ricky's clothes when he woke up and go visiting my friend Louise. She took him in and fed him and was concerned that the neighbors would file child abuse charges against me. She was a good friend and disliked the shadowy figure of the priest who visited me and ate the food that the Chinese cook gave us because he knew that we were needy.

My job at Eng's restaurant was very difficult for me because of my fractured skull and one kidney, and it was wearing me down.

My boss was always insulting me and calling me "Dumb, Dumb". I suffered for my children because there was no support from their father.

I had another friend, Leo, who witnessed the abuse that the boss gave me. His advice was save some money so you can get out of here and go home. His motto was "Don't Whine and Stay—Whistle and Walk Away".

My friend Barbara and I were targets for the abuse. One day they had a meeting and it was discussed. After the meeting Barbara and I quit. There was to be no change and the abuse got worse.

I applied for another job in a local restaurant. The conditions were worse for me. It was an exclusive place owned by a husband and wife. They knew who the good tippers were. The wife worked as a waitress. Guess who served the good tippers and important people. The cook hated these people and he said the conditions were the same all over. We not only waited on tables, we vacuumed and cleaned the restaurant after it closed. I went home with very little money. At least at Eng's I had some money at night.

I had rented out my house in Babylon and sometimes renters moved out and I could not pay the mortgage. It was obvious to me, even though I was brain damaged that the priest was only going to take care of himself, not us.

Sometimes someone gave us a basket of food and I tried to hang onto sanity.

One night there was a severe snowstorm. It was very common upstate to have 14 to 16 inches of snow. My daughter, Barbara, and Ricky and some neighbors shoveled snow for hours to dig out my car.

I got a phone call from the priest begging me to come to his luxury pad and help him.

My friend, Louise, who was very wise, told me if I left the house in my car after everyone shoveled me out, she could no longer be my friend. She saw Father L was a sneak and came to visit with his coat collar up and would not socialize with anyone.

BARBARA'S SCHOOL

I enrolled Barbara in a Catholic Academy with tuition of $30 per month and we had to purchase uniforms. Coleman Academy was an exclusive school way beyond my means. I wanted the best for Barbara but she did not like the school at all! She and her friend, Liza, were starting to run wild. There was an older boy, whom I saw was too old for Barbara, and I called and that ended. I used to make her take Johnny with her and really forced her into a role that belonged to me.

She dropped out of that school and went to public school.

RICKEY'S JOB AT THE GAS STATION

Rickey was out of school and got a job at a gas station. I used to go to see him on payday and he always gave me some money. He used to take us to Van's Ice Cream Parlor for ice cream sundaes when he had money. He had assumed the father role because there was no father role model. My family was torn apart. We had left a nice home in Babylon to a low down life style. At one time the community back home respected us. My children had piano lessons, nightly Rosary and now we lived below poverty level. I paid a heavy price for my sins. I just wanted to go home.

DICK'S VISIT

One night when I came home from work my husband was there. My children were all excited to see their father. They kept bragging about how he spent $60 on groceries! My poor Ricky walked him to the bus station. It broke my heart when I saw what little attention he paid to Ricky. This man was unable to love. He showed no emotion for our children or me. There was no doubt in my mind that this man, that I had married at 16 years of age, could not feel compassion or love for anyone.

What a pathetic sight it was for me to see my beloved Ricky trying to get close to this man who was his father. After he left I needed time to recover.

My mother decided to visit for a week. We were so crowded in the two-bedroom apartment, but mother was the boss. After all the years of neglect she said that she would baby sit for me.

I used to buy day old cakes and goodies for my children. Mama decided to hide them from my family. She called them gluttons. Another testimony of the sorrow I felt. My mother was also a cold person like my husband. It seemed like I had married my rejecting father and my emotionless mother. I call it "Writing the Same Story With a New Bic Pen". The story remains the same.

All these experiences made me decide to go into the "Healing Professions". I was and am a Wounded Healer. I quote from Schuller "Every experience has value if we can transform the scars into stars".

My mother wanted to get away from home and my sister's demands on her for money. She told me that my sister used to knock on the windows late at night demanding money. One of the excuses mother made for this behavior was "your sister is sick, we must excuse her". My mother never seemed to see the poverty that my children and I were living in.

FLORIDA TRIP

My so called friend the priest, would not meet with my mother but he decided to take me to Florida to see my friend from Eng's who had moved there with her two children.

Now that Mama would baby sit my four children, I was free to take a weeks vacation, which I sorely needed.

Father L drove non-stop to Florida. He decided to take a room in a dingy hotel for one night. I promptly fell asleep and was awakened by an exterminator spraying the room for bugs. Father L told me he wanted to punish me with the dingy hotel room so I would appreciate the next hotel.

I was heartsick and all I wanted was to return to the person I used to be before I let the "devil" into my home and my heart. I was paying a heavy price for my sins. The priest and I never had sex because he said he was <u>celibate</u>. This confused me also, but since my logic was gone I still trusted him.

I tried to escape from him in St. Augustine. I got out of the car with my clothes and ran to the bus terminal. He was not through with me yet. He followed me until I got into his car.

We went to a hotel and I took his car to the beach in Daytona. I wanted to kill myself and escape from the life I was forced into.

One night he threw open the door to the hotel room and I was passed out on the bed. He said, "Father Leonard came to see your Sunday school teacher". I was so sick and demented that I felt Father Leonard was there observing my behavior. The priest was very sick and demented and wanted to punish me in every way he could.

He claimed to be celibate and did not have sex with me. However, he told me about the fellow priests who were anything but holy. I wanted to go back home and return to the person I used to be before 666 Albin Avenue took possession of my soul. Back home at Hanratty Street, appropriately named, Ricky made friends with Billy and his mother lived in a house which was very neglected, since she too was raising a family by herself.

Barbara was starting to get into trouble with her friend Lisa. Her family was nice people but Lisa was running wild. It was time for me to move back home. I had some money, I am not sure how. I made the move on my own, without help from the priest.

MOTHER'S LONG, LONG VISIT

Mama extended her visit for another week. She asked me what I was doing upstate. I told her Father L promised to take care of my family since Dick was gone.

I was very confused and sick. One night I gave my mother the priest's phone number to call him and ask him for his explanation of why I moved. He said: "Your daughter followed me and I was trying to get rid of her". For the first time my mother seemed to feel some compassion for us. However, she decided to leave. Although she never showed any emotion, I am sure one of her rosaries was heard in Heaven to deliver me.

I lived in fear of telling this priest that I was leaving. My son Ricky refused to come with us. The priest drove us to the bus station and showed no emotion, no concern. My three children and I boarded the bus and left for home. I cried all the way on the bus until we reached Penn Station.

Louise, my one friend, asked me to stay. I kept telling her about my good friends at home. She said all these things change with time.

Now I was leaving a sorrowful town with one child missing, my first born son. Ricky was not coming with us. He decided to stay with the Beaver family. They were really a downtrodden group of very poor people.

As I rode on the bus I cried and cried. I cried for the person I used to be before the devils entered my home.

HOME AGAIN

We arrived at my dream house in Babylon to find utter ruin. The tenant had flooded the furnace and the ceilings were all water soaked. The house looked very small to me. My dream house was now a nightmare. I was returning to my home with one child missing, my first-born son.

I went to visit my friends, Blanche and Mike, and they found it very funny that the former tenant had put a casket on my lawn. Yes, my life was a joke to them.

Next I called my friend, Anne, and told her I was home. She seemed to be glad. She gave me a "coming home" party at another friend's house. I was introduced as the "Mystery Guest". It was a great reason to drink and be merry. The invited me to a church meeting. The pastor asked me to donate my time to a cake sale to bring in revenue for the church. Of course I agreed. I did not know how to say "NO". Thus the title "A Room Without Roaches, Please". I not only had low self-esteem, I had no self-esteem.

My house was a wreck and I had very little money, no car no phone and no help from my friends or family. I did have job at Pioneer Diner, which provided food money for my children. I placed my baby in a nursery so I could work. Every morning I took a cab with John to go to work. He and I had to wait in the diner until the nursery opened. My other two children were enrolled in the local school.

Here I was, in terrible financial difficulty, trying to repair my home and running a church cake sale. What a fool I was!

ROOM RENTING

In the meantime, I knew that I had to do something to survive. So I ran an ad in the paper to rent rooms in my house. I rented my two rooms up stairs for $25 a week while I slept on the couch. What a sad sight my home had become. The people who rented from me were low lives and drunks. Many times they would move out in the middle of the night and not pay me. They had to share my bathroom and there was no privacy for my children and me.

I hired a plumber to put in a shower and toilet up stairs so they would not have to come into my house. My fair weather friend Anne's husband, Jim, put up a wall in my living room, so the room renters could not see into my house. They now had a private entrance. He charged me for the day's labor and the material he used. They were heartless knowing we were starving. You see they had enough money and were untouched by the poverty they witnessed. You will remember that they were the same people who partied and ate and drank in my house when we had money.

This should have taught me a lesson. But I did not learn. I felt they were good Catholics and meant well by me. Now life had changed for my family and me. We were no longer respected in the community. My children picked some bad playmates.

My neighbor Mike came to visit on Sunday morning to show us the donuts he bought for his obese wife, Blanche. He used to swing the donuts in the face of my children, but never offered us one.

RICKY RETURNS

My son, Ricky, came back home to find his room rented to a tenant for $25 a week. Three rooms were rented, all except one that was occupied by Robert and John. I slept on the couch. Ricky and Barbara slept in the basement. "A Room Without Roaches, Please".

I met a man, called Joe, who tried to finish the basement. He also laid a cement walk outside. Mike and Blanche thought it was funny to watch him trying to help me. He had 4 children of his own and his wife left him with the care of his family. Joe had a good sense of my poverty. Blanche and Mike called him "Rotten Suchs" because he did not make a good appearance. He had a good heart, which they did not.

Now my friend, Mildred, whose husband drove the death car and my dearly beloved, Anne, came to visit me. They went into the basement and saw Joe putting up walls and walked away with gratitude that this was not happening to them. Jim, Anne's husband, worked two jobs and was always busy with his friends improving their houses.

The tenants I rented to moved out in the middle of the night without paying their rent. One tenant got drunk and fell down the stairs. I asked Ricky to drive with him to the hospital. When the nurse asked him what happened, he falsely stated that Ricky pushed him. Another tenant used to knock on the walls of his room. I could hardly sleep because of the noise.

One day my husband came to visit and saw the living conditions but would not contribute to this horror scene.

Here I was with a fractured skull, loss of hearing, only one kidney and trying to survive and keep my children intact.

Mama came to visit and slept in one of the empty rooms. She used to get drunk and walk to the corner store and buy beer and drink it in the woods nearby. I never spoke to her about her drinking. She had kidney failure and I felt terribly sorry for her. Unknowingly I became the mother of my mother. But any meal I made she criticized and put me down. "A Room Without Roaches, Please". I was walking through life with a steady injection of unworthiness.

Ricky used to hang out at Argyle Lake. Barbara followed her brother and they both spent time there daily.

ARGYLE LAKE

One of the reasons that I bought this house was because I saw this beautiful lake and some water falls with lovely flowers and ducks swimming in the lake. My mother and stepfather used to like to have picnics with my children at this site.

Suddenly Argyle Lake turned into "Needle Park". The teenagers used to go there, play hooky from school and drink and do drugs. This area of my life is very difficult to write about.

Barbara met a young boy there, with whom she fell in love. Timmy was a serious drug addict. I knew nothing about drugs so when she brought him home, I was unaware that he had a problem. Today, if I close my eyes, I can see him sitting on my couch very pale and sad. Barbara told me he lived nearby and slept on a couch in his home. His mother and stepfather were abusive to him.

My own life was in shambles around me. I called a local newspaper to tell them the story of my non-support. He asked me to meet him but I could not take time off from my waitress job.

I was starting to drink very heavily now. I tried to create a new reality. I was in and out of blackouts, partly because of alcohol, but also because of the severe auto accident head injury to the left side of my head, which is the hemisphere that controls logical functions. Until this day my head is dented on the left side because there was no money for doctors or medical help.

I used to ride down to Argyle Park to try to get my children to come home. They used to call me the "White Narc". Of course no one knew where my children were. They were hiding out there doing drugs and drinking.

I had Robert and John at home and they were subject to watching their brother and sister strung out on drugs.

Barbara's boy friend, Timmy, told me his mother was in AA and that his stepfather was also in the program. I met his parents and drove them to an AA meeting.

My home was in complete disarray. I could not count on my mother for help. She visited weekly and sat on the couch saying the Rosary. Ricky was very abusive to me. Ricky spit in my face and hit me on the left side of my head, which is where I was damaged in the auto accident. I was forced to tell Ricky he had to leave.

When Ricky left my house, I watched him walk down the street with his long blonde hair, and I felt like my heart would break. I wondered what had happened to our home that used to be a holy, prayerful place with all the members saying a nightly Rosary. All my dreams went up in smoke. I was drinking very heavily and trying to keep a job as a waitress.

Every time a tenant paid me $25 for the room rent, I ran to the street to buy food for my children since their father never sent a penny home after he left. All I could do was go to work and come home to an empty house. Barbara was baby-sitting her brother so I could work.

One day Barbara told me that her brother, Ricky, was on heroin and sleeping in the park. I knew nothing about heroin or drugs. When I went to work in the Pioneer Diner a lawyer always sat at my table and we became friends. I told him about the candles and spoons in my house and he confirmed the fact that my children were using heroin. I took Ricky back home very strung out. I called my doctor and we tried to admit him to a hospital. No one would take him, not even the emergency room. In those days it was difficult to get treatment for drug addiction.

I called his father to please come and help me. He came and saw my son who was almost in a coma. He sat on Ricky's chest and asked him why he didn't drink instead of doing heroin. Then I called a priest to come and give my son the Last Rites. He said: "We don't do that anymore" and said a prayer and left.

I took my son to a health center and they gave him methadone every three hours. I called his father again to help me. I could not go to work and leave my children because now Barbara told me that she was pregnant. She used to run away to her father in Brooklyn and then down to her boy friend's house and come back home to have her baby.

My first grandchild was soon to arrive, and I was told not to let her in my house. I did not listen to anyone.

I adored my daughter, Barbara, and blamed her boy friend for her drug addiction and her pregnancy. I put a deposit on a beautiful crib for my first grandchild and when I went to pick it up, the store told me a girl and her boy friend told the store her baby died and got back the deposit. Who the girl was remains a mystery to me. So I called Timmy's mother and told her off about her son. This was very unjust, but I always blame other people for my daughter's behavior. I was in complete denial about Barbara's problem.

Now at this time I had two young children who were not safe in the house.

SUMMER CAMP

I sent my two younger children to Camp Alveria for $150.00 a week to get them out of the drug-affected area called home. Ricky was lying on a couch and Barbara was pregnant. What a sight! Mother paid her weekly visit and said a Rosary for us. There was no financial or emotional support from the church or my church friends. When the good times were over they all left.

God sent an angel to my home in the form of a Jewish woman, Sandy Z. She asked me if I would go to an AA meeting with her. This woman was my first introduction to any knowledge about alcoholism or drug addiction. I learned a lot about mind-altering drugs and their effect on the family. I knew that I needed to save my two youngest children from the drug-affected behavior of my son and daughter. When my money for Camp Alveria ran out, my children came home to the environment that I had tried to get them away from.

One day I sat crying in the church and the pastor came over to me and asked me why I was so sad. I told him that my two older children were on drugs and I was afraid to go to work and leave them at home alone. The pastor told me to bring them to his church in Deer Park because they had a day camp and he would be glad to have them in his day camp. I felt like this was a miracle to help my family. I offered the pastor money and he refused saying I had suffered enough.

John and Robert were able to go to day school for the whole summer and I could go to work with an easy mind, knowing they were safe. As I look back over my life now, I know that God was watching over me.

DEER PARK DINER

Now that my children were safe during the day, I would go to work at the only trade I knew, waitress work. There was a man, who owned a body and fender shop in Deer Park, who took a liking to me. My boss and he were good friends. I tried to get him to hire Ricky in his shop but he would not hire him. I barely made enough money to buy food. My tips and the rent from the rooms helped us to survive.

My mother liked to visit weekly in order to get away from my sister's abuse. My mother told me that my sister used to come in the middle of the night and knock on Mama's bedroom windows asking for money. Mother felt that my home was a safe place. However, my four children were too much for her.

My friend Tony invited Mama and me out for dinner. We went to a Chinese restaurant and Mama would not eat anything but apple pie. Tony had a fancy car with light on the floor and Mama sat in the back seat. As I have stated previously, Mama's kidneys had gone out. I knew that, when Tony opened the door to let her out, he would see urine streaming on the floor. I never disrespected my mother and made believe nothing happened.

Mother used to like to visit weekly and be the boss. My son, Robert, was her favorite. She made him a special milk shake because she felt that he was too thin. I am sure that she meant well but the other children felt rejected. I let her be the boss and I am sure that she thought that I was retarded. She came when she pleased and left when she pleased. Whenever I asked her to stay, for instance I prepared an Easter dinner but I had to work, she would decide to leave and get my neighbor, Mike D'Perro, now deceased, to drive her since he drove a cab in New York City. Mike and Blanche were my son John's god-parents but never did a thing to help us.

The Deer Park Diner was going under financially due to the boss Jimmy's alcoholism. At one point in time, Jimmy had two diners, but alcohol and women had sent him into bankruptcy. He was just hanging on by a thread. I had to go to his other diner on Deer Park Avenue to get food to cook for the diner I worked in. When the cook came in he asked me where the food was. I jokingly said, "Did you bring it?"

He kept hiring new cooks because he had no money to pay them. One cook said to me: "My wife doesn't believe I'm working here because every time I ask him for money he threatens to fire me".

I never got paid but I could live on the tips I made each day. My son John and I used to sit at the counter and eat in order to break even for the money he owed me.

Jimmy had a charismatic personality. Everyone liked him, but he was drunk everyday. His wife found out he had a girl friend. One day his wife came with his two children and started throwing things all over the diner. The kids kept screaming for their mother to stop breaking things. It was a sad sight to see what alcohol had done to this once prosperous man and his family.

The last day I worked there, the electric company turned off the lights. We had some local merchants who asked me what was wrong. I lied and said, "It is a power failure". They said: "That is funny. My business is next door and there is no power failure on the block".

I do not know how Jimmy's story ended. Rumors said that he and his girl friend went to jail. Tony and he gambled and although Tony did not drink, he was a heavy gambler. But despite that habit he was very generous to my family and me.

TONY AND HIS FARM STAND

Tony was a friend of my boss at the Deer Park Diner. Tony's wife was in Pilgrim State Mental Hospital due to the loss of their little girl. The child was run over and the wife blamed herself and so did Tony. She had a nervous breakdown and was institutionalized with no hope for recovery. They had another son whom Tony adored, also a compulsive gambler like his father. The son persuaded Tony to buy a farm stand in Westbury. He purchased it very cheaply and remodeled it. The farm stand was almost half a block long and he needed many workers to help him. He hired cashiers and also my daughter, Barbara, and my son, Robert, to work for him. There were too many exits so it was impossible to see that no one stole. Late one night, Tony's son stole a lot of fruit from his father.

At this time I had a job as a waitress across the street from my friend Tony's farm stand. I over heard the son's plans to steal from his father. Tony wouldn't believe me and after a while he lost his house in Deer Park and was sleeping on a door in his farm stand. Another addictions story.

The son got a job as a horse trainer at the racetrack nearby. I saw Tony one day selling potatoes from a truck. I believe he was homeless.

Tony had bought me a huge engagement ring, which I had to sell to repair my house. I guess it was good that I sold it because he wanted it back and would only have gambled it away. I don't know how Tony ended up.

PHOENIX ARIZONA

One day I got a Christmas card from Arizona. Ricky had left the house and I didn't hear from him. The card said "Someone Loves You". When I opened the card I found it was from the Maricura Chaplain of the jail there. My son was in jail. I went to an AA meeting and some men put me in touch with a priest in Arizona. I did not know how I was going to get there. NO MONEY! No family support! Friends gone! I thought that if I could borrow the bus money from my friend Anne I could get my son out of jail. I went to Anne's house and asked for $100. She said: "I have to ask my husband, you come back tomorrow and I will let you know". The next day I returned with a ring to assure her that I would pay her back. She said: "Jim said no, if it were for sickness we would give it to you". I went away heartbroken and sad.

My sister came forward and bought me a plane ticket. We both went to Phoenix. I went to the local church and spoke about my problem and he heard my confession. We were staying at a local hotel and we got a pass to visit Ricky. My sister made a scene at the prison because she wanted a chair to sit down. My son was terrified that the prison guards would take their anger out on him. I begged her to stop causing problems. Her behavior was very inappropriate and she got the attention of all the guards. My son, Ricky, and I were very embarrassed by her behavior. I went to a lawyer and my son was released from jail. It was a minor charge and when he was released he turned to me and said: "I would have gotten out anyway without you". I said: "Next time you will". My sister, Ricky and I went back home. I picked up my two youngest sons from Tony's house and my friend, Sandra, a nurse, suggested that I take Ricky to a friend of hers who was a judge. The judge told my son, Ricky, that he had imposed on me enough. I was willing to go back to Arizona with Ricky to meet his conditions of probation, but the judge told him to go on his own. He did as directed and came back home. I was happy to have him because he appeared to be drug free. His father came to the house and offered him a job with the shipyard. Ricky left home to go and live with his father and his father's latest girl friend, Diana or Helen.

Helen and my husband had a residence in Brooklyn. She had children from another union and Dick was accused of fathering one child who was retarded.

At this time Dick and Ricky were working together and Helen needed a baby sitter because she drank heavily and went to the local bars. She had two baby sitters who were sisters. Marie and Julie were mentioned in the first part of this story. They lived with their mother, who was a single parent taking care of a small building in a run down section of Brooklyn. They claimed that while Dick was working on the ships, Helen used to come home drunk and never paid them for baby-sitting. They were both used to abuse from my husband, but out of loyalty to me, they came to the hospital when he was dying and stayed by my side.

When Marie was baby sitting for Dick and Helen, she met my son Ricky. She used to run away from home to come to my house on the island. I really loved this little broken sparrow. She was very good to me and she truly loved John and Robert. She used to try to breakup their fights. I always encouraged her to let them fight it out.

FIRST GRANDCHILD,
MELANIE HEATHER

There was a famous song at this time called, "I've Got A Brand New Pair of Roller Skates" etc, etc. Barbara was pregnant and she and her boy friend, Jimmy, were both MY actively using drugs. Barbara was in labor and I had no heat or hot water, so we went to my friend Tony's house to let Barbara wash up and I drove her to the hospital.

I stayed in the Chapel praying for my daughter and all of a sudden Timmy's mother came and tapped me on the shoulder to tell me Barbara had a baby girl. I rushed up to see my daughter and my grandchild. Melanie was a beautiful child. I was so happy that everyone was alive. I went home to prepare a room for this tiny baby. Her beautiful crib was waiting for her in Barbara's old room.

I fooled myself into thinking that everything was going to be all right. My Jewish friend, Sandra, told me not to let Barbara in. She seemed to be able to foretell the heartache that we all would suffer.

I was the main support of the family. Timmy's mother and father brought some used hand-me-down baby clothes to the hospital and never contributed anything else to their grandchild.

My friends came to see my beautiful grandchild and they enjoyed teasing me because I was always bragging about what she could do. Most babies did the same things but my Melanie was special. I decorated a room for my beautiful first grandchild while I slept on the couch, just as I did at my mother's house. "A Room Without Roaches, Please".

Barbara kept running back and forth between my house and Melanie's father's house. I carried a heavy cross trying to support all of them as a waitress. There were nights when I went to sleep and woke up to find my tips gone. I would then go to a gas station with a dollar to get some gas. The owner would laugh and ask me if I was going to New York City. I barely made it to Westbury where I had a job in a diner. I knew I did not have enough gas to get home, so my boss let me get some gas after the dinner hour was over.

On the way home I stopped at a store to get food for the family and baby food for Melanie. What a poverty driven existence! But I was happy to have my family with me. I was the sole support of the household. No one contributed a dime to help me out.

My mother came to visit every weekend and got drunk. My house was her "runaway" place from the financial and emotional abuse of my sister. She liked to visit my neighbor's, Blanche and Mike, and they drank together.

My life centered on my mother and my children. I was ending my days on a couch because that was the only thing I knew.

BARBARA AND TIMMY'S MARRIAGE

My daughter, Barbara, and Timmy got married and moved to Commack, Long Island. My mother and I went there to visit my first grandchild. I brought rolls and food. When we got to the apartment the cops were arresting Timmy. Robert and John witnessed the arrest. I wanted to bail out Timmy but I believe his mother got him out of jail. I always felt sorry for Timmy because he was a pitiful sight. He was very pale and drug addicted.

Not long after he was arrested they lost the apartment and Barbara came to live with me. Now I had Barbara, her husband, their two children, and my children. We had a full house. Imagine this during frequent visits by my mother. My mother seemed to want to come visit when the house was full of people and children. She was very fond of Robert and felt that he was too thin, so she made him special milk shake and he in turn loved her. She also bought him a bike so he could deliver newspapers.

I had a friend, Helen J. who gave me the name of a priest, Father Tom Hartman, who counseled people. He had an office in the rectory in Seaford. I told him all the things that were taking place in my home and he felt a deep compassion for me. He and I became friends. When I asked him to help my daughter, Barbara, he told me, "Help is for those who want it, not those who need it". He is a good and wise priest. He frequently called me by phone to ask how I was. He was a great help to me during this period of my life, for which I am very grateful. I guess he knew I was having a nervous breakdown, while my friends and family did not notice how much I was suffering.

Father Tom Harman was a young priest when I met him, and my only true friend at that time. Later he returned to academia and became a psychologist as I did. He is now on television.

My house needed a great deal of work and Ricky asked me to sign the house over to him. He said I could live there and go on welfare. With no financial support, I had struggled to keep the house. De ja vu, this was an echo of his father who had asked me to let him and his girl friend, Helen, and her children move in and take over the house, because, according to him, I was incompetent to raise our four children.

I thank God for His grace. I was advised not to sign over my house. Despite my poverty I hung on to the house. This was my dream home. Now, many years and tears later, my lovely statue of Saint Anthony still stands there.

Later in life my son, Ricky and Maria got divorced.

TIMMY'S BIRTH

Before the birth of her second child, Barbara and her husband and my beloved Melanie moved into an apartment not far from me. Barbara entered a hospital in Seaford where the baby was born. He was named Timmy, Jr. for his father. I stayed up all night decorating a bassinette for Timmy with green material. My friend, Dottie K., let me use her sewing machine. Timmy and Barbara took the baby home to their apartment. He was a sickly child from birth. Whenever I went to visit the place was crowded with drug abusers. My son Robert visited them and came home brokenhearted over the drug scene.

It was not long before they lost the apartment. I was devastated when I saw their things packed while little Timmy, Sr. was showing me his new blue shoes. I don't think either parent was in reality.

Barbara came back to live with me and I gave Barbara and her children my large up stairs bedroom. Again, as in childhood, I slept on a couch in order to accommodate the family. Barbara's husband went into a drug rehab program. She used to write to him often. Now my house was bursting at the seams, but I was very happy. My sons, John and Robert, really loved Melanie and little Timmy.

At Christmas I went to the Korvette store, where I charged "Minnie and Mickey Mouse" sheets' and all kinds of toys. I bought a bike for John and left it in the yard while I tied ribbons between my house and a tree in the back yard.

My son, Robert, joined the Air Borne and left for military service. This left a hole in my heart because Robert and I were very close. He had been a big help to Barbara and me in raising her children, Timmy and Melanie.

RICKY AND MARIA'S MARRIAGE

Maria was in love with Ricky. He met her while he was living with his father in Brooklyn and working in the shipyards. They used to run away from Brooklyn and come to my house. On one of their visits they brought me a dog. They called him "Shit Face" because they found him digging into garbage cans in Brooklyn. We renamed him "Pal" and all the family fell in love with him.

He was totally untrained and unmanageable. He would jump up and eat off the table. He would break through the screen door and follow the "Good Humor Ice Cream Truck". The driver would never give a child an ice cream cone, but Pal got an ice cream cone and took it home to eat on my steps. Pal used to roll over and sing with Johnny and Robert. One day he disappeared and we looked and looked at shelters and houses but could not find him.

Ricky and Maria decided to get married. They had a small ceremony in her mother's house in Brooklyn. I am sorry that I did not attend, but I did not want to have to see my ex-husband and his current girl friend. Ricky looked handsome. Barbara adjusted his tie but she did not go to the wedding either. I am not sure why.

MARIA CAME TO LIVE WITH MY FAMILY

One day in Brooklyn, an angel in the form of an army recruiter, who persuaded him to join the army, approached Ricky. At this time Maria had given birth to their son, Thomas. Ricky did not want to leave Maria in Brooklyn, so Maria and baby Thomas came to live with me. There was hardly any room in the house, but there was always room in my heart for my family.

Now as I write in the later years of my life, I wonder why they have no contact with me.

My mother came to visit every week despite of the fact that the house was so crowded there was no room for her, but I made room. There were meals to be cooked for all the family, but mother did not like to cook. She sat on the porch and said the rosary. When the noise became too great she went to visit Blanche. My mother and Maria did not get along. They were jealous of each other. Mother complained that Maria would not let her watch her favorite television shows. Every day, when I got home from my waitress job, I heard all their complaints.

Barbara was seldom at home. She was living back and forth between Mary Flynn's house and my house. The Flynn's house was where she preferred to be because Melanie's father lived there.

My house was a circus of people but we were happy. I barely made enough money to pay for the mortgage and buy food for everyone. Waitress work was all I knew. Everyday I came home weary and worn out trying to survive and keep my children alive. I refused welfare help because they wanted me to sign my house over to them. Also, it was a matter of pride, so I overworked and kept things going as best I could.

MY SECOND GRANDCHILD, THOMAS

Ricky had joined the army and left his wife, Maria, and their son, Thomas, with me. I loved Maria and Thomas, but I was so weary from working all kind of hours that I regret that I did not spend more time with them.

Maria liked to listen to Christian Broadcasting. One day she told me she wanted to become a Catholic. I introduced her to Father Bill Bricotti, a priest from Wyardonel. He baptized her and Thomas. When Ricky returned home on leave she told him the good news. Ricky was assigned to Germany and decided to take Maria and Thomas with him. I was sorry to see them leave.

There was an emptiness in my heart because Maria had become my daughter. Another loss to be sustained.

JULIE—MARIA'S SISTER

Julie was a sister of my daughter-in-law Maria. I did not get to know Julie very well, much to my sorrow. She was a waitress like me, with two children. She wanted to become a Catholic and I'm sorry I didn't help her to achieve that.

When my son Ricky and Maria returned from Germany, my mother and my children couldn't wait to see him. He now had three children, Thomas the first born, Wendy and Chrissy. Ricky told Chrissy that I was his mother and her grandmother. She said, "I don't like her". Ironically she became the closest of all my grandchildren and had kept in constant touch with me until today.

Julie was a single parent struggling to survive and support her two children. They came to visit and all stayed at a local hotel. I really wanted them to be in my house, but it was too crowded. Julie's boys were very active and the situation was compounded because John, my baby, was over active and not too well behaved. Julie moved to Brooklyn to live with her mother. One day, Julie's mother committed suicide, leaving Julie alone in the world. No one knew the exact circumstances of Mrs. Rice's death. It was supposed that she drowned herself. Her body was never found. To commemorate her memory Ricky sent money from Germany for a headstone in the cemetery although there is no body buried there. I said the family was doomed for tragedy from the womb to the tomb. They never had a chance for a good life. They were born in poverty and died in obscurity.

BABYLON DINER

My daughter, Barbara, and I got jobs as waitresses in the Babylon diner. Barbara and I worked different shifts so our children were not left alone. My mother's visits were less frequent now when we needed help to baby sit. The two Greek owners liked Barbara but did not like me.

Melanie was in first grade. My son, John, was doing poorly in school and getting into trouble. His school had no mercy for him or me. One teacher especially did not try to understand John's loss of his brother, Robert, and the fact that he had no father and a mother who had no time to give him. We were a broken family but no one noticed or cared about us. Most of my fair weather friends were not around. Poverty had set in. My player piano no longer played. The party was over. All the friends fled the scene.

After my son, Robert, left for the army, Barbara's son, Timmy used to play soldier. He really missed Robert and my son, John, and I had come to depend on Robert so his leaving was a great loss to the family. He offered to stay with us but I encouraged him to get his own life and I sent him off with $100 check and concealed my broken heart.

CHRISTMAS

My daughter, Barbara, and I were both working at the Babylon Diner. I was losing it, and the Greek owners did not like me. They gave me very few tables so I had very little tips. I had a charge account at the Kornette store and I ran up my charge to buy presents for John and Barbara and her children, Melanie and Timmy. At Christmas we all went to Woodside to take my mother to the circus and a Christmas dinner. When I got home I fell into an exhausted sleep.

I awoke up the next morning and went downstairs. All Barbara's Christmas clothes were on the floor. She and her two children were gone without a clue as to where or why. John and I looked at each other in shock and wonder. I was brokenhearted. I saw Melanie's school bags on the kitchen chair. I left the school bags on a chair in my kitchen hoping my daughter and my grandchild would return. My son, John, was at a loss, also. He adored Barbara and had become attached to Melanie and Timmy. Another loss.

We learned that Barbara had taken her children and gone to live with a girl we worked with, named Sue. She was an alcoholic and later died of alcoholism.

MULTIPLE SCLEROSIS SOCIETY

I saw an ad in the paper for a job at the Multiple Sclerosis Society. At this time there was a government CETA program to provide single parents and poor people training to qualify for positions for jobs through workfares.

June R. was the woman who interviewed and hired me. Six of us disadvantaged people were hired.

After Barbara left I had really bad problems with my son, John. He associated with a bad group of people. He was always in trouble in school and disobedient and disrespectful at home. One day the police arrested him for a minor offense but the handwriting was on the wall. John was in trouble. He went to court and the judge sent him to Sagmore Psychiatric Hospital.

Now my home was empty. I walked from room to room to mourn my children and my grandchildren.

SAGMORE PSYCHIATRIC

My son John was taken from me and was court ordered to a psychiatric hospital called Sagmore. When I saw him he was medicated and he seemed resigned to the fact that he was in a lock-up ward.

As we entered this hospital there was a large painting of a campsite, which had the words, "Hello Mama, Hello Papa, Here I Am At Camp Granada" printed on it.

I was heartbroken as I saw my son so sick and out of it. My friend Mike Green drove me to the hospital to see my son. After every visit I came home to an empty house. This was truly a season of sorrow. Walking through each room of my empty house, I remembered when my family said a rosary every night and we all went to Mass and Communion.

My son John said the hospital was a mad house, like the movie "One Flew Over The Cuckoo's Nest". When my friend and I went to visit John, he told me they were so crazy that when one boy fell asleep another urinated in his mouth. A man working there told me that weird things happened there. He also told me that it was a good thing that my son was so big, because inmates would beat him up just for the "Hell of it".

My insurance plan at the M.S. society would cover his hospitalization. I called the town of Babylon to find about another placement.

SOUTH OAKS HOSPITAL

I pulled some political strings and had my son transferred to South Oaks Hospital. One dreary morning John was admitted to South Oaks in Amityville. I had graduated from this hospital some years ago as an alcoholism counselor. My two sons were at my graduation, and one year later my last child was there.

What a cruel joke. After counseling many clients, now my child was in a lock up ward. Every time he acted out he was placed in a straight jacket, and they also gave him thorazine.

I pulled some rank, and called the doctor and told him I would sue if they would not do without the thorazine and the straight jacket. They needed to know that I was concerned about my son and would not tolerate their abuse.

I went daily to see him and I walked the streets in a very dangerous neighborhood in order to visit him. He seemed to be better adjusted and had a good attitude.

My son Robert, who had joined the Airborne, came home unexpectedly, and brought a bike for his brother. When he came into the house, I had to break the bad news to him and told him that Johnny was in the hospital. We took the bike there to surprise him. He was very happy to see his brother and me. We took the bicycle back home until he was released. It didn't happen that way. He ran away from the hospital and came back home.

His behavior was worse than ever. The treatment plan was no help at all. John was heartbroken over the loss of his sister, his niece and his nephew. I was not a full time mother because of my job. His grandmother never came to my house any more.

One day he confessed to me that he felt it was his fault that his father left. He was a baby of one year old. Imagine this child blaming himself for being born.

We were no longer respected in the community and my house was sorely in need of repairs. John's behavior became worse and worse. The roomers were not reliable with the rent, and my daughter never came to visit or bring my grand children to see me.

I was still holding onto my low paying job in the Multiple Sclerosis Society.

ALTERNATE SENTENCING PROGRAM

My job was counseling the clients who were diagnosed with M.S. My caseload was very heavy and the primary interest of the M.S. Society was to raise funds, not counseling. However, I stuck it out for the hospitalization and insurance. Many clients came before me and I helped them with their grieving process.

Since the main interest was fund raising, I needed to find some volunteers to help me with the counseling groups I was setting up. I started many groups for my people, but I was sorely in need of help. In order to do a good job, I looked to volunteers.

One day I saw an ad in the paper for a new program that was starting. It was an Alternative Sentencing Program, which was started to eliminate jail crowding. In lieu of prison, the felons were assigned to me. This was a big help and I gave the many assignments to train them for a new life. Most of them were alcoholics and drug addicts.

The court system gave me about seven clients to work off their time as volunteers. I was privileged to see their recovery.

Since I wanted to be of the utmost help to my people, I went back to school and my boss gave me the summer off to go to Rutgers University where I got a degree and did research on alcoholism. My friend Mike G. stayed at my house and took care of John for the summer.

I was also enrolled in Adelphi and got another degree after securing my G.E.D. God looked down on me, and school was a nice diversion for me. God had given me a vacation from the sorrow of my life.

My dream house was a living nightmare. God was watching over my life. It was not a pretty picture. My son was not getting any better, and neither was I.

MY SURGERY

While I was attending school and working, I had a placement in a hospital and I got very sick.

I went to a doctor who was recommended to me by a friend, and she put me in Huntington Hospital for a D.N.C. After that operation, she took me back for a hysterectomy.

One again, God smiled on me, and this surgery was covered by my insurance. My education was temporarily interrupted, but I was able to resume school after a period at home. My daughter lived five minutes from me and never visited me. My reason for staying in Babylon was disappearing.

I had a friend and lover who saw the sorrow in my house and he asked me to be engaged to him. He was a family man and could not understand how my husband could have left us to starve. He had a wife and took care of her until she died of cancer. He was very kind to me, but he did not like my son John.

Someone was robbing the rooms that I rented and people were moving out without paying their rent. I had no friends left and had no desire to stay in my once "Dream House", which was now a "House of Horrors". It was time to move on.

LEAVING BABYLON

Several real estate companies came to my home and since I was so stressed out and mentally broken down I did not know the value of real estate. A friend advised me to wait for a while since real estate was going to boom. I did not listen to any advice at all and sold my house at half of the total value. My children came to say goodbye to the house they had never visited for years. My son Ricky took all the furniture and no one asked me where I was going. It seemed like no one cared where I was to live and just left me and the house behind. I left a lifetime of memories that day.

When my children were small, they carved their initials in a tree. By the time I sold the house, the tree had grown and we had outgrown the house. Most of my dreams went up in smoke. There was no reason for me to remain in Babylon. John was gone I'm not sure where. I was still trying to hang on to my house and my memories of days gone by. I really had nowhere to go.

BAY SHORE RENTAL

I rented a studio room in Bay Shore. One room with kitchen, bedroom and bath combined. It was a sad dreary place. However I had a hope that my daughter Barbara would visit me there since she lived close by. I had raised my two grandchildren from birth. But she and her children never came near me. So I felt like this was not a place for me.

One night my neighbor Mike, John's Godfather, came to the door with John. John was burned over most of his body. Instead of taking John to the hospital, which was much closed than my house, he dumped John off and left without saying a word to me. I told John we must get him to the hospital. He was severely burned and very sick.

It was a dark rainy night, and I had an old car, which barely ran and had defective windshield wipers. John gave me a hard time about going to the hospital. I finally got him into the back seat of the car and laid him down. The rain was so heavy I could not see the road. I flagged a truck down to help me. I was afraid John would die in the back seat. The driver went to put me in the car, and leave John there to die. I escaped this man and I prayed that my car would make it to the hospital. They kept him in the emergency room for hours after he was admitted. Then the police came and kept questioning him before he was taken to a room. I did not get much sleep that night but I went to work at the M.S. Society because I truly was dedicated to my job and my clients despite my problems at home.

After being diagnosed with M.S., many people came to me for counseling to help them through their adjustment and grieving process.

One man brought his terminally ill wife to me in a van because the neurologist charged $100 per visit and then sent them to me to discuss ways they both could cope with the disease. At this time there was very little hope and no cure for M.S.

My boss had very little compassion for the clients. Her concern was fund raising not the welfare of the clients. She would take phone calls and call me and say "someone fell off their toilet" and they need to speak to you. She made sick jokes about the clients. However she had a dynamic personality and the hierarchy was very impressed by her. They did not know how little she cared for the clients. Although she was one of the most ineffective people I knew, they gave her a big promotion. An example of the Peter Principle.

The handwriting was on the wall. This was a prelude of what was to come.

My clients truly loved me. I was told my boss was very jealous of the love the clients had for me, and the clients who were assigned to me from the prison system.

At a dinner for the patients she and her bosses sat at the podium and she assigned me to the back of the room and to take the clients to the bathroom. I felt the Holy Spirit speak to me and I knew that it would not be long before she would fire me.

LOST THE JOB BUT I FOUND MYSELF

One morning at work, a senior boss came into my office and told me I was fired. My friend Mike G., who had worked with me as a volunteer, and did the work of three people, was in shock. Mike had delivered wheelchairs and helped me with the prisoners on work release and knew I worked long hours and helped many people. My family had also helped me care for the handicapped. Mike helped me gather my books and things together and my boss kept talking. I lost control of my one kidney and wet myself in panic. Mike kept saying, "Piss on them, let's get out of here". We had to walk past a typist and the secretary who was drunk. I left in shame and sorrow.

I would not miss the staff but I would sure miss my clients.

Now I was on the unemployment line collecting $150.00 a week and feeling sorry for myself. I called a friend of mine and told him my sad story and he told me that there were 100's of people who were fired today. He also said that when God closes a door he opens a window. I went back to see the person that fired me but there was no response.

I had moved to Huntington to be closer to my job and I shared a home with a woman who was very spiritual, that is, until she drank. When she drank all bets were off. She used to fall asleep in the bathtub and I had to turn the water off. It was like being back with Mama, without the abuse but she was great company and we had many laughs.

Her mother called from Scotland. She bragged to her mother about my job as Director of M.S. She gave me a party at her home when I graduated from Adelphi and received my Masters Degree. After my party I told her she better call her mother and tell her that I was fired.

We had fun together and I paid my rent. We joined a writers club and did a lot of dancing. My friend R was very intent on marrying me and he told me to come and live in his son's room and finish my doctorate degree. It sounded like a good deal as I had sold my house and John was not living with me.

MOVING TO MASSAPEQUA

I bade Sally good-bye and gathered up my few belongings to go to live in Massapequa. R had his daughter L living with him and his other daughter, Mary, came to visit and have dinner. I believe Mary took an instant dislike to me because I have more education than she had and her mother died a tragic death with cancer.

The house was a dark dismal place. I used to walk several blocks to Mass at St. Rose Di Lima every morning. R was heavily into valium addiction. His daughter, the nurse, got him really strung out. He was functioning on his job but seemed to be in a zombie state. Both daughters were getting plenty of money from him. It was to their advantage to keep their father on valium.

The both resented me and were grieving for their mother. I could not concentrate on my doctoral degree because I was so unhappy in this dismal atmosphere.

One day I saw a little bird fluttering for his life. Against his protest I took the bird home in a box and fed it. The bird died and I died also. God spoke to me because I was a wounded sparrow also.

John was not welcome in the house because he refused to cut his hair. He was living in a furnished room in Babylon. I used to take him food weekly. John was very generous with his food and shared it with another boy.

The owner of the rooming house was a member of the local church. He had every room in the house rented. John had paid his rent and I left food in the house for both boys. The "holy" one ate the food and claimed John did not pay him his rent, so I left a check for him in his Bible and he claimed that he did not get the check. So much for "holy" people.

JULIE'S SON'S DEATH

I went to South Oaks for counseling. A young girl cried when I told her my story. She called me to tell me that she never called a client but wanted to call me and console me.

One day the phone rang and my son Ricky called me to tell me Julie, my daughter-in-law's sister, had a house fire and her two sons were burned to death. I had a new car but no idea how to get to Rhode Island, where the deaths occurred. God guided my car and I went to console the family. Julie had been a waitress like me, and was living in an impoverished apartment when the fire broke out. Her two boys were sleeping there. She said she could hear their screams but could not get into the room where they were burned to death. It was a heartbreaking time for all of us. I don't know how I was able to drive home to my prison cell in Massapequa. God guided my car and I went home to a silent house where no one spoke to me.

MOTHER'S DEATH OR MURDER

I had been trying to reach my mother by phone and letter. I sent cash and checks to my sister's house with my friend Mike Green. My sister cashed my checks to my mother without my permission. One day I went to a Lutheran Church and two girls prayed about my mother. They asked me to write a letter to my mother despite the fact that I was abused by her throughout my whole life. I wrote the letter but then I called the Lutheran Church and told one of the girls that I did not want to send the letter and hurt my mother. She told me to read the letter to her. I did, and then a miracle happened.

I went to 8:00 Mass in Saint Rose Di Lima Church and told the priest my story about my mother and the fact that my sister would not let me see my mother, but always sent out a big black dog on me.

My friend, Mike G., had throat cancer and spoke through a tube, but he always was a dear friend to me. Mike brought my gifts to my mother, but my sister never gave her the gifts or the money I sent.

When we went to my sister's house, as usual, she would not let us in to see my mother. By chance I met an old man crossing the street and he said, "Old lady carried out of house". That was all he said and disappeared.

Mike and I went to get information from Dr. Perry, who was my mother's physician, but he had retired. Next we went to three funeral parlors to see if they had had a service for my mother. There were no records.

My next step was to visit my mother's next-door neighbor, Mrs. Powers. Mrs. Powers informed me that my sister used to come and demand money from Mom. She also used to cash Social security checks.

I knew there was foul play here. I went to the rental office. They told me that the apartment was rented to a man.

Now I knew why my sister kept me from seeing my mother.

I went to the local police station.

They found a death report. It stated that, on August 4 of the previous year, my mother was deceased of unknown causes. That meant that my mother had been dead one year while my sister would not let us into her house. She had told visiting relatives that my mother was in Ireland.

The police report further stated that she had been taken to Campbell Funeral Parlor and the body had been taken to Calvary Cemetery. There was no record of a ceremony at Campbell Funeral Parlor.

I said I was a daughter and asked how this could happen without my knowledge. Mr. Campbell informed me that this happens all the time, especially when money is involved.

When I returned to my dreary room in a sick home in Massapequa, my cousin Arthur called me. He said he had tried but could not reach me. He knew my mother was dead and he had investigated the matter. He told me about some money that was left to me by my Aunt Elsie. I knew nothing about this, nor did I care. I was heartbroken over my mother's death or murder by pills.

Once before, when my mother stayed with my sister during my stepfather's funeral, my sister refused to let any one see my mother. She had her spaced out on lithium. This was even more suspicious.

My cousin, Arthur, said my aunt had left me some money and gave me the name of a lawyer who had my Aunt Elsie's will. I went to the lawyer and he showed me a $3,000 check left to me by my aunt. I said, "I am not here for money. I want to investigate my mother's death."

He felt concerned because my Aunt Elsie trusted him. He then showed me that my sister had signed my maiden name, JoAnn Gallagher to the inheritance check.

After he was certain that the signature was not mine, he wrote a letter to my sister saying he was sure she made a mistake when she cashed my $3000 check. He inferred it was grand larceny. My sister sent him $3,000, which he gave me and apologized for not checking the signature since my Aunt Elsie trusted him to do the right thing.

I went home and talked to a missionary priest who said he would conduct a Memorial Mass for my mother. People came from the

Lutheran Church with guitars, and a friend, Rita Camera, sang songs. I wanted it to be a High Mass so I bought two Styrofoam crosses and my children pinned a rose on one cross and my grandchildren pinned a rose on the other cross. The crosses were both placed on the altar with a prayer for my dead mother.

Many people told me that they had never experienced a service anything like it before. They had come to comfort me but they had received a great blessing and comfort.

After the service we had a party at my temporary home in Massapequa.

None of my fiancé's family attended the Memorial Mass or came to my party. The handwriting was on the wall. The Lord was telling me to move out of this dreary atmosphere.

DISTRICT ATTORNEY'S OFFICE

Because he considered my mother's death suspicious, the lawyer suggested that I go to the District Attorney's office in the district where the crime occurred. I did as he suggested. The District Attorney told me that because my mother's death was suspicious, I could have an autopsy done. He gave my file an index number and said that within a reasonable time limit, I could open up a case to have an autopsy performed. He advised that I had better prepare for more pain.

I left his office knowing an autopsy could not bring my mother back so I did not request it. I went home to my prison cell like room.

FARMINGDALE

The family that lived with in Massapequa did not like me there. The lonely man was trying to buy the love of his daughters, Mary and Loretta. He gave them large sums of money. He gave one daughter money for the down payment on her house. The other daughter was on some kind of drug and slept most of the time. He had a large pool in his yard and they came and swam and went home when he came home from work.

One day Mary's husband called me on the phone and accused me of wanting R's money. His house was a shack and if he had any money it was not apparent. I was not in desperate need of money; I had my own money from the sale of my house. I really just needed some love and kindness. I re-did the kitchen with my own money and bought nice curtains to brighten up the place, but the sickness and silence remained heavy on my soul. This was not the place I needed to be.

My daughter and grandchildren did not visit me and my son was not allowed to visit because he had long hair. I had no purpose and my soul was in jeopardy. I felt like I was in the valley of the dead. I attended Mass and Communion daily and felt that God was speaking to me to get out of this prison cell like room.

His daughter gave R. valium and he was like a zombie. I tried to help him but to no avail. After predicting that his daughters would carry him out feet first, I knew that I had to leave and get another place to live.

I found an apartment in Farmingdale where rent and the cost of living were low. My low self-esteem was no self-esteem.

My new living quarters were on the top half of a two family house. I had a bedroom and a living room combined with a kitchen. This was not much better than the room I had in Massapequa except that it was close to a church to which I could walk every day.

One day as I was walking to church I noticed a young man in a car following me. Because of the years I had worked as a waitress I was familiar with most of the curse words because many of the cooks spoke Spanish.

He followed me in the car to the church. I walked over to his car and told him "I don't think you are looking for me son". I asked him to come in to the church with me. He came in and knelt beside me and said "I have not been in a church since I was a small child". This was a Divine appointment. Another mini-miracle on the highway of life.

The landlord's house was in an area zoned to be a single-family dwelling and was being inspected because of the second floor apartment. He had cut a portion of the floor out so I could look down into the apartment down stairs. He said that was only temporary until the Housing Authority had made their inspection.

Months went by and the living conditions were intolerable. The family that lived down stairs was constantly fighting. Again I felt it was time to move on, although I did not know where to go.

I had a part time job at a facility that housed retarded people. I saw much cruelty there. Patients were suffering severely at the hands of attendants.

We attendants were trained to modify the suffering patient's dysfunctional: My heart broke for one man who was abused by his "so-called caretaker" when he lost control of his kidneys.

I came early one morning to find the caretaker "hung over" from all night partying.

The attendants had a racket among themselves. They took money for new clothing and bought second hand clothing for the patients. There was no one to whom I could register a complaint. I used to leave the facility crying for the abuse to the patients. I knew that I should no longer work there and I quit the job. I was very lonely and lost in Farmingdale.

John came home to live with me in this apartment. The owner did not want two people living there. My son was very disturbed. I asked an AA member to take John to the Farmington meeting but he was not interested in him. I had tried everything humanly possible to help him.

Paying his court fees, therapy at South Oaks, AA meetings and loving him with all my heart and soul were of no avail.

John's behavior was very bad. I knew he was sick but I was powerless to help him. I told him he had 30 days to get a job and straighten out. He was unable to do either. One day John came home and practically broke up the apartment. Although it broke my heart I told him to leave.

As I was running to church I found a red rose. I was sure someone had dropped it. When I called my friend Rita, she said the rose was from Saint Theresa. Saint Theresa promised to send a shower of roses from heaven whenever a prayer was answered. Apparently God meant to heal my broken life and me. It was not my son John's time.

SUPREME COURT

One day I received a call telling me that I should come to Brooklyn for an interview for a position in the Supreme Court system. I did not remember applying for the job. Apparently God was calling me to work with the Intensive Supervision Program in Brooklyn. They did a film on my technique of counseling and because I had several degrees in alcohol counseling (Rational Emotive Therapy Behavior Modification) and was in the doctoral program I was hired.

One day, as I was taking the bus from my home, I met a woman at the bus stop. I was not sure how much the fare was. She looked at me as if I were from Mars. I explained to her that I was from Long Island and we got into a conversation about the Island. She knew my mother and had lived in the same apartment complex. We started talking about my childhood days. I told her about my mother's death and she said she had heard some rumors but declined to talk about it. She seemed to know a good deal about my sister's abuse and the fact that she rented my mother's apartment but she said she did not want to be involved because her son was killed also. We both had a heavy heart.

While I was on my way I had the opportunity to see a homeless man sleeping on a grate to stay warm. God gave me the gift of being able to give him some money and prayers. This man was Jesus in disguise and I pray never to pass by any such person.

The Bible story of the Good Samaritan tells of a man left at the side of the road by a robber who beat him half to death. Many religious leaders passed on the other side of the street to avoid having to help him. Then a man from a neighboring but discredited place (Samaria) came by. The Good Samaritan bound up his wounds and took the victim to an inn to recover. God sends his followers to help others along life's highway.

I accepted employment as the Supreme Court and spent ten years working with high-risk felons. I saw much recovery on my caseload.

One day a guard was shot by another guard and I knew it was time to give my notice and leave. I had done a good job while there and received many awards for my service. I gathered my belongings together and they gave me a nice party.

God led me to Florida and I wrote a book on the homeless. As I write this I am alone and without family. However, I have a ministry in the streets with the homeless boys and girls. As I minister to them I pray God will send someone to help my son Johnny who is missing as of this writing.